NOËL KINGSBURY

Plants to transform
your garden

WARD LOCK

A Ward Lock Book

Cassell
Wellington House, 125 Strand
London WC2R 0BB
www.cassell.co.uk

A Cassell Imprint

Text copyright © Noël Kingsbury 1998
Illustration copyright © Ward Lock 1998

Distributed in the United States by
Sterling Publishing Co. Inc.
387 Park Avenue South
New York NY 10016–8810

British Library Cataloguing-in-Publication Data

A catalogue record for this book is available
from the British Library

ISBN 0–7063–7711–7

Designed and typeset by Lindsey Johns at
The Design Revolution, Brighton

Printed and bound in Spain by Gràficas Reunidas

Contents

Introduction

What makes a garden successful? Is it a distinctive design, well-planned borders, carefully laid out paths and walls and the existence of a few spectacular plants, or is it the presence of features, such as pools and fountains, urns and archways?

In truth, all these aspects contribute to making a garden successful, but, if pressed, most people would put planting at the top of the list. Plants are essential to a garden, and avant-garde attempts to do without them always end up looking absurd and sterile, the butt of sharp-tongued reviewers at garden shows and of a derisive general public. Plants are the raison d'être of a garden – indeed, they are part of the definition most of us would give of a garden. No matter how elaborate your balustraded terrace, no matter how expensive the cherub-infested antique urns adorning it and no matter how clever the design of the garden, ultimately, most of us will judge it on the planting.

When we stop to look at someone's garden, rather than just walk past it, it is usually a plant or a combination of plants that stops us in our tracks. It is only then that we begin to look at the other features of the garden, whether or not it is well laid out or has an interesting sculpture or an attractive terrace. Even if it has none of these things and is only, on reflection, something of a jumble of good plants, it has still made us stop and look.

Many of us are unhappy with our gardens. The borders may look great in spring but lifeless and dull later in the year. There may be bare spaces under trees, or there may be a pond whose outstanding characteristic is a bare concrete rim. You may baulk at the thought of redesigning the garden, let alone paying for someone else to do

so, or at the prospect of trying to improve it with new features of wood and concrete. The easiest way to transform any garden, however, is with plants, and it is far and away the cheapest way, too. It can sometimes also be quicker than you might think possible.

This book is about how to select plants to bring life, colour and joy to your garden. It is based on the belief that a few well-chosen plants can make or break a garden, and they are well chosen because they look good and grow well in the conditions that nature (or the architect or builder) has created in your plot. First, we look at the reasons people are often unhappy with their gardens and at how to analyse the faults, which is an essential first step in making any improvements. Then we look at the plants themselves. We look at plants that are grown for the colour of their flowers or leaves, or for the elegance of their foliage. We consider how different species can contribute to the garden at different times of year. We assess the use of plants in containers and in conditions that seem less than perfect, in particular shade, which nearly everyone has at least a little of. We look at 'instant' gardens, and how you can effect a transformation in as short a time as possible. Finally, we include some practical guidance on replanning and replanting borders and other garden features. The emphasis throughout is on building on existing gardens, on analysing their good and bad points and on improving on what is already there.

The shaft of light created by a stem of *Onopordum acanthium* makes all the difference to this border.

About the Plant Directories

Most of the chapters end with a directory of plants that are relevant to the topic covered in that chapter.

The growth form of the plant is indicated – tree, shrub, herbaceous perennial and so on – with the perennials, the form may be indicated as erect growing – that is, plants such as aquilegias and meadow rue (*Thalictrum* spp.) that do not form clumps – or clump forming, as with geraniums. I have tried to give some indication of how much they might spread outwards. Size is given in the form height × spread. With many clump-forming perennials, the spread is, theoretically, infinite, so the average spread after three years is given.

The choice of the plants in most of these sections is a personal one, because in most cases there are so many possibilities. The selection is made on the basis that the plant will combine a definitely superior quality with reliability in the garden, and use in the smaller garden has been considered in all instances.

I have tended to concentrate on plants that, although readily available, are not the most common options, and I have included a few that, until a few years ago, were known only to connoisseurs but are now more widely appreciated. In some cases, supplementary lists of plants are included; these, too, are necessarily selective but will provide additional ideas.

A combination of strong shapes and foliage colour ensures that this area looks good for a long period. The flowers are almost the icing on the cake.

The role of plants

An ornamental garden is primarily a celebration of our love of plant life. Most of us start gardening with flowers, which have an immediate impact on us, just as they do on the bees and other insects for which nature designed them. Some of us like vivid colour, others prefer subtle shades. As we become more knowledgeable we often refine and develop our tastes, and we begin to appreciate that it is not just flowers that provide colour in the garden, but often the foliage and even the stems that are left bare in winter. Many gardeners go on to see beauty in shape and form – the elegant thrust of a branch, a distinctive outline or a pattern of foliage.

Our Love of Plants

The more we look at plants, the more we tend to see and the more we learn to look for particular things at certain times of year. Whereas once we may have noticed plants only if they had bright colours, experience teaches us that there is more to look for – the tones of fresh growth in spring, the luxuriance of foliage in summer or the seed-heads of perennials and grasses in soft winter light. While colour may seize the initial attention of the onlooker, it is often these other factors that give long-term pleasure to gardeners themselves.

Gardens are expected to assume an increasing number of roles. Magazines make us feel socially inadequate if we are not having a barbecue with the neighbours every other night, environmentally irresponsible if we do not have a 'wildlife area' or philistine if we do not have some reference to garden tradition. But the fact is that our garden will not give us – let alone our friends and neighbours –

Above: A path lets you walk right through a planting, important here to enable you to experience the fragrance of the *Hesperis matronalis* in the foreground.

pleasure if we do not have beautiful and rewarding plants within it. Barbecues, nettles and mock antiquity do not a garden make. They are no more than accompaniments to good planting.

The Trouble with Garden Designers

It was not long ago that hardly anyone except the very wealthy employed a garden designer. Indeed, very few people even thought much about garden design at all. Recently, however, a veritable explosion of books, magazine articles and television programmes – matched by an explosion in the population of garden designers – has made us all very aware of this aspect. Perhaps too aware, for many people have begun to feel inadequate if they do not have a garden that looks like something out of a magazine or television programme.

Garden design, rather like interior design, has fads and fashions. For a few years the historical look is 'in', and the gardens at shows and exhibitions sprout mock ruins and pseudo-classical urns. Then 'hard landscaping' takes over for a few years, and the plants retreat before wooden decking and little brick and concrete walls.

Next it is the turn of the wildflowers, and it becomes impossible to tell the difference between the show garden and the waste ground at the end of the road.

The trick of garden design is to overwhelm by the immediate impression that is created. It is difficult to argue with a harmonious and practical distribution of borders, paths and paving, and a good garden designer will make everything look so well ordered. Bad designers may hide their inadequacies behind attention-grabbing sculptures or plant 'styling' that will last for only a few years. A closer look will reveal that such gardeners tend to use the same plants in their gardens again and again. Often they will use the same plants as each other, or the same plants as whoever is the most influential of their number at the moment. Some of the greatest reputations have been founded on no more than about 20 varieties of plant. The truth of the matter is that all too many garden designers do not seem to be very interested in plants.

Design skills are not easy to come by – indeed, it can be argued that you either have them or you do not – and if you want to transform your garden but the thought of all those pieces of paper and drawing lines and angles to scale fills you with dread, then forget it. Concentrate instead on choosing some good plants. They will give you more pleasure in the long term and are more likely to be more remarked upon.

Selecting and Buying Plants

There is now an enormous selection of plants available to us. The basic range of varieties offered by garden centres (which is often huge anyway) has been augmented by those offered by specialist nurseries, whose products can be obtained at the increasing number of horticultural fairs and shows or sent by carrier, even across frontiers. The choice of plants with which to transform your garden has never been greater, and neither has the selection of books, magazines and other media to help you make the choice.

It is always good to have a clear rationale when you are buying plants, otherwise you may end up with what is sometimes nothing more than a mismatched jumble of varieties, each exceptional and choice in its own right but bearing no relationship to the rest, so that you finish up with a botanical garden run riot. The sections into which this book is divided are intended to help you develop that clear rationale.

Choosing plants is a highly personal matter, of course, but it is wise to be aware of some basic guidelines. After all, the plants will have some say in the matter.

SIZE: HOW BIG AND WHEN?
All too often, the decision to buy a particular plant is regretted after a number of years, when the plant sprawls expansively over everything else within reach.

Books about plants usually give their ultimate size or the size they achieve after a given number of years – so make sure that you know which one it is. Often, books give only the height, but it may be the spread that proves to be the crucial factor. Some reference books do give height times spread after 5, 10 and 20 years, but they are few.

It makes sense to acquire only those plants whose ultimate size will not cause problems. It is, however, often possible to limit the size of plants by pruning or cutting them, in the same way that hedges are kept cut to size. Large, unruly shrubs – mock orange (*Philadelphus* spp.), for instance – can be pruned hard immediately after flowering to limit their size or even be kept trained to walls or fences. It is possible to enjoy the foliage of large trees if they are coppiced every few years (by being cut back to the base) and allowed to resprout as a shrub. It is not uncommon to treat eucalyptus in this way, but the process could be applied to many other species.

SOIL

It is widely known that certain plants will never grow well or may even die in certain soils – rhododendrons in lime-containing soils, for example. It is worth taking the time to find out what grows well in your soil, for you will save a lot of trouble if you concentrate on what will flourish naturally rather than trying to change the conditions to suit what you would, in ideal circumstances, want to grow. Roses are a case in point. They really do well only in deep soils, and they quite like heavy clays. Growing them on shallow, sandy or dry soils is a waste of time, and it would be better to look at all the other, equally attractive alternatives that by nature grow better on these soils.

CLIMATE AND IRRIGATION

Plants are highly sensitive to climate, and, as with soils, it is better to select those that will thrive readily in your garden than to try to change conditions to suit the plants. Irrigation in particular is the main means by which gardeners try to overcome drought, but it is becoming increasingly impracticable in a world where there are greater and greater demands on water resources. There is a large number of very attractive plants that are drought resistant, so with careful planning there should be little need to reach for the hosepipe.

Winter cold is the other main limiting factor that climate imposes, and a more absolute one even than that of summer drought. Many gardeners derive a great deal of satisfaction from growing a surprisingly wide variety of plants in places where they might not be expected to succeed. Common techniques include growing them on sheltered sunny walls, insulating the roots in winter with straw or bubble plastic or digging plants up and overwintering them under cover. Many gardeners will have neither the time nor the inclination to go to such trouble, however, and they should concentrate on those species that are known to be 'bone hardy' in the area in which they live.

The chapter on 'Problem' Sites looks at the potential for choosing plants in what can be difficult garden conditions, such as cold and drought.

Flowering shrubs like this rhododendron make a one-season splash, but can look dreary for the rest of the year.

Assessing your garden

Before you can transform your garden, it helps to be able to analyse it critically in order to identify the problems. You may feel only a vague sense of unease that it does not give as much pleasure as it ought, or you might visit other people's gardens and see things that make you think: 'I could do that in my garden.'

Visiting gardens that are open to the public is a particularly good source of planting ideas and an excellent way of learning about new plants. Once you have decided on the aspects that need improving – and perhaps made a note of what you see as the problem areas in your own garden – you should keep an eye out for comparable areas in gardens that you visit to see how the problems have been overcome and with what plants.

This chapter aims to help you look at some of the particular problems that commonly arise in gardens, and to encourage you to ask the kinds of questions that will enable you to find appropriate and successful planting solutions to those problems.

Borders that Lack Colour or Real Focus

It is not uncommon to find a border in a garden that would be perfectly acceptable in a public space or look quite outstanding next to a supermarket car park but which, although tidy, is far too dull for a garden. This is usually because it is composed solely of shrubs, which fill the space neatly but have a short flowering season and look very dull for the other 11 months of the year. Plants with more impact are what is required.

Plantings like this often benefit from the removal of a proportion of the shrubs and their replacement with perennials or other more carefully selected shrubs. However, be aware that gaps cut into dense shrub planting can look very bare, with lots of dead stem visible in the plants that are left. Consider the possibility that, having started on the slippery slope, you may decide that what remains looks hideous and that the survivors may not regrow new foliage from the bare branches.

In this situation, there are two possible courses to follow: one is to cut the surviving shrubs down to the ground and let them regrow; the other is to plant new shrubs rather than perennials (which will die down to ground level in winter) in the cleared spaces to hide the bare branches as quickly as possible.

The kinds of shrub that are used in landscaping are great space fillers, but they are often rather amorphous. Using large-leaved perennials or shrubs or stylishly architectural plants can make a lot of difference to the overall impact, too. Not many are needed to breathe new life into a dull border.

Keep a record of what looks good when. This can be used as a guide to help you decide what plants should come out and at what times of year their replacements should flower or look good. How quickly will the replacements fill the gap, or are you prepared to live with the gaps for the sake of having more space to grow lower growing but much more colourful perennials or annuals?

Think not just about flowers, but also about foliage colour and form. If all the existing foliage is green, how about a lightening touch of yellow or variegation, or a darker touch of purple? Is there a need for strong foliage shapes or a plant with a completely different shape, such as bamboo or a palm or a yucca?

Colourful Borders that Lack a Sense of Structure

Borders are often colourful but chaotic, lacking either a sense of structure or a cohesive theme. Such borders are usually the result of years of impulse buying in nurseries and garden centres, as new purchases are 'fitted in some-where' without thought to the overall appearance of the bed or border. All the plants may be perfectly healthy and flower well and there may even be flowers all through the year, but the result is, nevertheless, chaotic.

Colour by itself is not enough. Strong shapes (delphinium and lupin spires, poppy bowls) add another dimension to early summer exuberance.

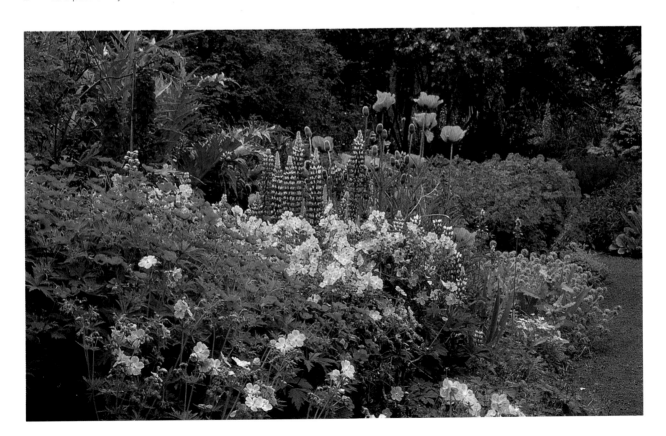

There is no doubt that as far as borders are concerned, the simple idea is often the best. This is the kind of border that needs a determined hand, for there will probably be a lot of plants to dig out and give away – a boon for friends, relatives and local charitable events. There may be certain plants in the border that you like and that can be used to create a theme, and this will involve removing anything else that flowers at the same time or that has a colour that clashes with your favoured plant. Alternatively, you may be more ruthless and decide to develop a colour theme, taking out anything that does not fit in with it and replacing these with plants that do.

Borders of this kind often look a mess because little attention has been paid to plant and leaf form and shape. Consider how you could introduce a number of foliage plants, perhaps several individuals of the same variety, and scatter them through the planting. This can be particularly effective with small evergreens such as lavender (*Lavandula* spp.) and cotton lavender (*Santolina* spp.). A traditional but highly effective device is to use an evergreen such as clipped box (*Buxus* spp.) and to include plants at regular intervals along the edges or through the middle of the border. Any such regular planting along or through a border can work wonders in tying it together.

WHAT TO ASK

Keeping a diary or recording changes with a series of photographs is essential if you are faced with a border that has no formal structure or theme, so that you can make sensible decisions about what should stay, what should be thinned and what should be removed entirely.

What are the plants that are really worth keeping? When do they flower? What else could be planted to complement them? What detracts from them?

Is there a need for strong, decisive foliage shapes or plant forms? Could you improve things simply by repeating one plant with attractive foliage at regular intervals?

The chapter on Creating Interest with Architectural Plants will help you develop ideas about plant form and foliage.

'One-season' Borders

Some people are what might be described as 'one-season' gardeners. They get very excited in, say, spring, making sure that they have plenty of bulbs, then perhaps reach a peak of enthusiasm in early summer, but cannot keep their interest going for very much longer. From midsummer onwards a gradual disarray overtakes the garden, and by early autumn things have become so dull that they cut down as much as possible to ground level. Such gardeners are missing out on a lot.

Golden *Rudbeckia* 'Goldsturm' and a mauve aster (*A.* 'Little Carlow') make for plenty of colour late in the season, along with the silvery foliage of *Plectranthus argenteus*.

Ideally, most of us would like our gardens to look good for as long as possible, which is not an unreasonable desire because there is a very wide range of plants to flower from late winter to late autumn. Given that there are plenty of evergreens available, too, there is little excuse for a boring garden in winter either.

The horticultural industry is not very good at selling late-flowering plants. This is partly because many such plants are perennials that grow rather too tall to be displayed conveniently in pots, and partly because autumn is a difficult season to market plants, even though it is the best time to carry out planting. The best way to get late-season ideas is to visit gardens open to the public that are known either for their wide plant collections (arboreta in winter always have plenty of interesting ideas) or for displays of herbaceous perennials, which reach a grand finale in early autumn. Make a note of names and buy the plants by mail order from specialist nurseries or by visiting late-season plant shows and sales.

WHAT TO ASK

A useful planning exercise is to keep a diary of what plant flowers where and when in the garden. Alternatively, you can take several photographs each month so that you have a visual record of different parts of the garden throughout the seasons.

Whichever method you adopt, you will have a useful record of seasonal interest, which will enable you to identify gaps that need to be filled.

Look at the garden in the dull season and think about how a few new plants might improve things. Make notes. Now look through your notes when the garden is at its best. How many of those new plants do you actually want to include in the garden, given that many of them are not particularly exciting (and some are even downright boring) at other times of the year. You will have to work out a balanced compromise between the two.

The chapter on Impact All Year Round will give you ideas on making your garden an all-year-round one.

Bleak and Uninteresting Expanses of Lawn

All too often, gardens consist of apparently unending stretches of featureless lawn, which is not only uninspiring to look at but also time consuming to cut. The previous owner of your house might have had a passion for riding around on a mini-tractor, mowing the grass and possibly fantasizing that he (it is always a 'he') was driving a combine harvester across a wheatfield in Iowa. One solution to the dilemma is to create an 'island' bed, but it is possible that you do not wish to create more borders with shrubs and perennials, which will also involve maintenance.

There are two other possibilities, which will, in the long term, involve far less work. The first solution is to plant some specimen trees or shrubs; choose species with fine form that will look good on their own or in small groups and will break up the bleak expanse of grass. The second option is to let parts of the grass grow to create a wild meadow effect, to which you might add some robust wildflowers or perennials.

Island beds are usually planted with taller shrubs or perennials in the centre and progressively shorter ones towards the edge. Such beds are a very good way of showing off good plants, especially if something you are proud of is made the centrepiece. It is important that an island bed is proportional to the whole of the space in which it is put: if it is too small, it will look inconsequential; if it is too large, it will overpower the surrounding lawn.

If there is the space, specimen trees are an alternative to island beds. The ultimate specimen trees are those, such as the cedar of Lebanon (*Cedrus libani*), that grace eighteenth-century parkland; but they are for only the largest gardens and for future generations. There are, however, plenty of other smaller and more quickly developing trees that can be used as specimens. Elegant shape is the main criterion, or features such as gracefully layered branches, or perhaps spectacular and distinctive flowers. Some, especially those with a narrow shape, are best as a small group.

The wild meadow option involves turning part of the lawn over to a 'wild garden', which is cut only once or twice a year, with the grass allowed to grow long. Such a garden is a boon for wildlife, and the resulting butterflies and birdlife might be an attraction in themselves. Long

Small specimen trees, such as this *Prunus subhirtella* 'Autumnalis', are ideal for making
a dull expanse of lawn more interesting and eventful.

grass may look graceful and romantic in midsummer, but it can get untidier later in the year, and you will have to decide whether you can live with this. It is possible to make long grass look more intentional by mowing paths through it or by having the occasional, very formal feature, like a clipped yew (*Taxus* spp.) tree. It is also common practice for the area of lawn that is farthest from the house to be treated in this way.

If your soil is poor, it may be possible to replace the grass with a true wildflower meadow. Most soils are simply too rich for this to be a viable option, because tough grasses allow little else to grow. An alternative is to introduce some large and vigorous perennials that can compete with the grasses on their own terms. They will provide a striking contrast to the surrounding grass.

WHAT TO ASK

Do you want an island bed? Have you got time to maintain it? Bear in mind that an island bed needs to be planted with more care than a border because it has to look good from all angles – there is no hiding leggy plants at the back – and getting a good gradation in height from the centre to the outside is not always easy.

If specimen trees sound an attractive option, consider carefully how many you could fit in – the whole point of specimen trees is lost once they become crowded. Knowing the ultimate size is vital. Research them well, and plant only your absolute favourites. See the chapter on Specimen Plants for more information.

Could you live with a meadow in the garden? It will certainly save an awful lot of work, but it may not be practicable – and will certainly not be very attractive – if there is a problem with persistent and invasive weeds such as docks and nettles, which will make the area look uncared for. Is your soil noticeably poor? If it is, consider replacing the lawn with a wildflower meadow. If your soil is rich, you will have to be satisfied simply with long and only occasionally cut grass, which can be extremely attractive, especially when bisected with mown grass paths.

Structurally Important but Dull Shrubs

It is all too common for a garden to be dominated by large, mature shrubs that are genuinely spectacular but for a short period only, and that look thoroughly dull or even funereal for the rest of the year. Rhododendrons are one of the most common examples of such shrubs. In some cases it might be worth reducing their size,

although it may be difficult to do this without ruining their appearance. The best option is often to plant other perennials alongside them or to interplant them with other, smaller shrub species that flower at a different time.

Perennials have the great advantage of a seasonal pattern of growth that involves their starting off from ground level every spring, and most have a later flowering season than many shrubs. So it makes sense to plant tall-growing, later flowering perennials, such as asters, around and between dull shrubs. When the shrubs are in flower, the perennials will be only 30–40cm (12–16in) high, and when the perennials are in flower they will be between 1m and 2m (3–6ft) high, partially hiding and drawing attention away from the shrubs. If some of the larger ornamental grasses – *Miscanthus sinensis*, for

Evergreens can be criticized for being dull, but not golden variegated ones like this holly, especially appreciated in winter.

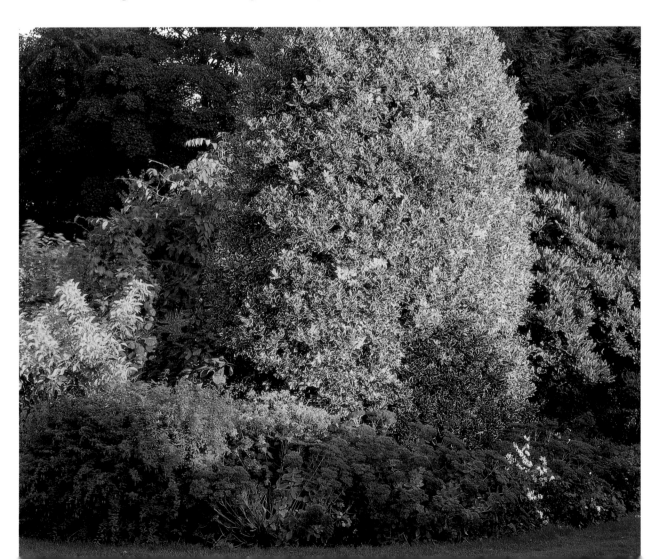

example – are used, then there will be interest well into early winter. Winter-flowering heathers (*Erica* spp.), hellebores (*Helleborus* spp.) and early bulbs around the edges of the shrubs are also worth considering.

Another option that is sometimes possible is to allow later-flowering climbers to scramble over the shrubs, much as they do naturally. Only light-growing climbers are suitable, otherwise the shrubs will be covered with a thick mat of stems and foliage and will be rapidly hidden. Herbaceous climbers (those that die down in the winter), such as the golden hop (*Humulus lupulus* 'Aureus') or the everlasting sweetpea (*Lathyrus latifolius*), are a possibility.

WHAT TO ASK

How much space is there around the shrubs for later-season planting? Are perennials going to be able to grow without being shaded heavily? If there is not enough space, it may be worth considering developing another adjacent area of the garden for interest later in the year.

When do the shrubs flower? Ideally, you will want a succession of perennials to carry on flowering from when the shrubs finish. Do any of the shrubs have autumn interest, such as colourful berries or leaves? If they do, think about late flowers that might combine well with them, such as violet and purple asters and yellow golden rod (*Solidago* spp.)

What about the winter? Evergreens can look very dull and deciduous shrubs unattractive at this time. Consider introducing some grasses, whose light and airy seedheads will provide contrast. Is there enough space for some winter-flowering heathers (*Erica* spp.) to grow around the shrubs? Turn to the chapter on Impact All Year Round for more ideas.

Highly Visible Key Areas

A garden may have lots of good plants and attractive corners, but if the key areas are dull or have received little attention for some years, then it will not be a success. The front garden may be bare or the view from the main windows of the house may be uninspiring. The problem may

be that there is too much bare lawn or too much dull evergreen planting. The garden may be suffering from the consequences of too much dense planting years ago, so that there is a thicket of tangled shrubs, none of which is giving of its best.

High-impact plants are needed – that is, plants that impress the visitor and will reward every glance from the window. Gardens with drab key areas can sometimes be greatly improved by the introduction of only one or two carefully chosen plants – specimen shrubs in a lawn, for example. Indeed, keeping it simple may often be the best solution, especially if there is a high level of planting in the rest of the garden.

If the problem is existing overgrown and dull planting, the first task is to decide what to remove. Ideally, replacements should not repeat the problems created by the originals – do not rip out a huge forsythia only to put in a philadelphus that will get to the same size in five years' time. Both plants flower for a few weeks and look grim for 11 months. Think instead about simplifying the whole planting scheme. A multiple planting of something with a long season, which you know you like and which does well in your garden, can often create more impact than a collection of different things. A bold swathe of ten evergreen ornamental grasses through a planting of multiples of three different heather varieties will be far more effective than one or two grasses scattered among small clumps of seven different heather varieties.

Using multiples of plants, especially smaller ones, is guaranteed to increase impact.

Half-hardy perennials flower for most of the summer and early autumn; these include osteospermums, petunias, nicotiana, verbena and cosmos. Containers can extend the theme of a border if it is too narrow.

Consider concentrating on extending the season of interest or choosing species with stylish foliage instead of 'nine-day flowering wonders'. A long-season, foliage-based planting can be particularly effective in key areas if it is combined with something more seasonal, such as hardy annuals, bedding plants, bulbs or flowering perennials.

Planting for key areas should fit in with the rest of the garden, or, if it is to contrast, it should be a contrast you feel happy with. You might decide to develop a theme that already exists elsewhere in the garden. If hardy geraniums do well, for example, carve out an island bed in the front lawn and plant out a whole mass of them. They will need something else with them to give a sense of structure – some grasses or clipped box, for instance – but you know that they will succeed, and you can probably propagate them yourself if you already have some growing.

The most important thing about planning key-area planting is to be bold and imaginative. The best effects often result from throwing caution to the winds.

WHAT TO ASK

Is it important that the planting is of interest all year round? If so, consider evergreens, but remember that plants that look the same all year can get jolly boring. Evergreens make a fine backbone to a planting, but some seasonal variation is important.

What have been the most successful plants in your garden? Consider using them as the basis for a key-area planting. Think about the most effective plantings you have seen in other gardens. If you do not want to copy them, think about the factors that made them successful in your eyes.

If you have some ideas about what to plant, how long will it take to reach the size necessary to fulfil its purpose? Something that takes ten years before anyone notices it rather defeats the object of key-area planting. By all means think about the long term, but such planting should be combined with varieties that will provide interest in the shorter term – perennials with trees, for example.

Left: Terraces and steps are one way to make a slope more manageable, but they are a good way of displaying plants too, allowing them to tumble down.

Above: Shade is brought to life in spring by bulbs and early-flowering perennials, like these *Anemone blanda* and hyacinths.

Places Where Little Seems to Grow

Nearly all gardens have at least one difficult spot where whatever gets planted seems to die, almost as if the soil has some kind of aversion to plants. Usually, the problem is caused by a combination of difficult environmental factors: the dry shade beneath trees or under the eaves of a house, or a hot, dry bank cut into subsoil. In general, plants need three things – light, water and nutrients – and if one of these is in short supply but the other two are plentiful, satisfactory growth is still possible. If two of the factors are inadequate, you will have great difficulty getting anything to survive.

The cross-hatching indicates deep, dry shade under a tree where little will grow.

Erect-growing shrubs, such as *Rubus* 'Benenden' (syn. *R.* Tridel 'Benenden') or the flowering currant (*Ribes sanguineum*), which tolerate some shade, act as a screen, hiding the bare patch.

Such places need not necessarily be barren. Given difficult environmental factors, such as dry or infertile soil, it may be worth trying to improve the soil, although on a steep bank, for example, this may prove to be impossible. Alternatively, you may simply prefer the easier option of using plants that are tolerant of the problem. You can usually find something that will grow in even the most difficult of circumstances, be it only ordinary green ivy – a dull plant is better than nothing at all.

If there is space, it may be worth considering treating the bare patch as if it were an eyesore and hiding it – for example, by planting some screening shrubs in front of a tree. If these are sufficiently eye-catching, your best hope is to draw attention away from the dull space.

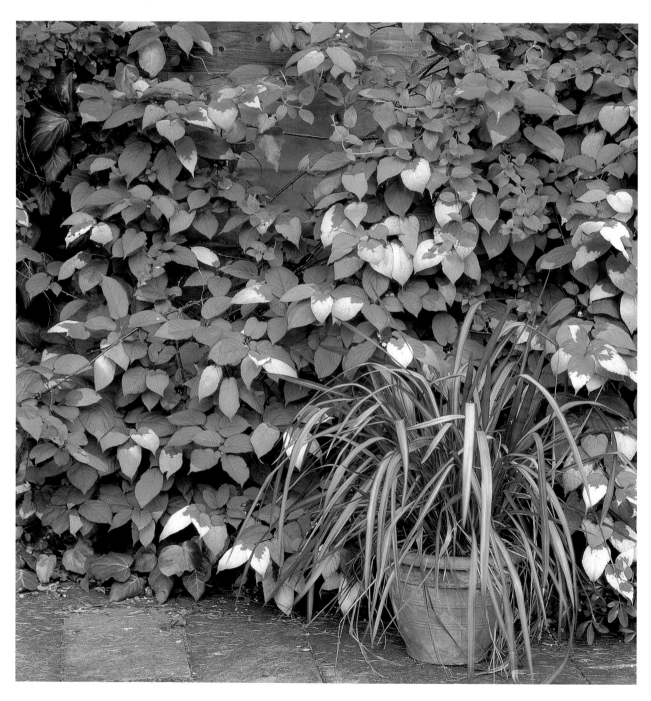

Containerized plants are very useful for quick and easy temporary colour combinations. The shrub is *Actinidia kolomikta*.

Garden centres and nurseries, to say nothing of reference books, can be great sources of advice on what will survive where, but only if you really understand what the problem is. Wait until the first rain after a dry spell, and go and dig a hole. If it is still dry, this may be part of the trouble. Is there rubble or subsoil, or are there tree roots hidden below the surface that may be the cause of the drought and impoverishment? Are there any worms? If not, the soil may be compacted or in bad condition. If there is some light, soil improvement may well make it possible for more plants to grow.

See the chapter on Shade for more on difficult shade, and the one on 'Problem' Sites for other areas which are often seen as problematic.

Bare Places Dominated by Walls or Fencing

Large expanses of bare wall or fence can often be unattractive, yet they can usually be covered with climbers or wall shrubs. If the soil at the base of a wall is dry or full of rubble, only the most tolerant species will survive, but, assuming it is not, there is scope for some genuinely creative planting. One of the great things about climbers is how many can be squeezed into a small space, and the results of mixing climbing roses, clematis and honeysuckle can be wonderfully romantic, as well as providing a long season of colour and scent.

Because most climbers need support, the surface will need to be covered with firmly attached trellis or support wires. If this is not feasible, then you will be limited to the number of climbers that self-cling by means of tendrils – ivies (*Hedera* spp.), the climbing hydrangea (*Hydrangea anomala* subsp. *petiolaris*) and virginia creeper (*Parthenocissus quinquefolia*) and its relatives. Such climbers do not damage plasterwork as is commonly believed; on the contrary, they help to protect it from the elements.

The self-clinging ivies and creepers are vigorous enough to reach the top of a two-storey building, given

time. So too are a good number of other large-growing climbers. If it is possible to attach support wires, you can train some truly magnificent climbers to a great height.

Wall shrubs are an alternative to climbers. Often, these are slightly tender species, which benefit from being grown on sunny walls, such as ceanothus, which will, incidentally, not mind being planted in rubble. If there is space, the shrub can simply be planted close to the wall and allowed to spread up and out. Given limited sideways space, it would be wiser to train the shrub against the wall, perhaps using trellis or wires to hold it in place.

Shrubs such as ceanothus and pyracantha are often grown on walls. In fact, it is perfectly possible to plant a much wider range. Untidy shrubs like forsythia and philadelphus can be trained to fences and walls, and if they are kept pruned this is a good way of growing them in a small garden.

How much space is there to fill? The ultimate size of the climber that is planted will need to relate closely to the available space. You do not want to end up with gutters or neighbouring trees clogged with clematis.

How much sideways space is there? Remember that many climbers, and wall shrubs even more so, are inclined to spread out sideways quite strongly. They can be fitted into narrow spaces, but only if you prune and train them.

What aspect is the surface to be covered? Is it shaded or sunny? Is there shade for the roots, which is important for many climbers, especially clematis? Is it exposed to wind, which may damage otherwise strongly growing plants? There is more on using climbers on walls in the chapter on Transforming Projects (see pages 148–50).

How much room is there for a climber to grow out from its support? Some climbers can be trained to grow very tightly, which is useful for narrow passages, for example. Only self-clingers like Virginia creepers and the smaller-leaved ivies can be trusted to do this naturally.

Overgrown Plants and Neglected Areas

Old gardens often feature huge shrubs that have long since exceeded the modest proportions that were planned by those who planted them, or they include borders where a number of the more aggressive perennials, such as Michaelmas daisies (*Aster* spp.) or golden rod (*Solidago* spp.), have formed large clumps at the expense of everything else.

Overgrown areas like this can often be salvaged, and they have the advantage that once the restoration work is done you have some mature shrubs that would otherwise take years to reach that size. It will nearly always be necessary to do some replanting, to introduce new life or to replace losses.

It is often wise not to remove too much of what are obviously overgrown garden plants straight away. Wait until they have flowered and you are sure that they are not worth keeping. If they are to stay, they can be trimmed back into shape.

When you come to replant such an area, you should aim to complement the existing planting with the new species you introduce, and to make the overall effect more exciting and attractive.

WHAT TO ASK

Once you have decided what to keep, you must choose some plants that will look good with the existing ones. Are there any combinations you have seen in other gardens that might be worth trying? Try leafing through illustrated plant reference books and imagine what might go well with the existing plants. At what time of year do these flower? How about selecting something that will flower, or be at its best, at another season?

It is also important to consider environmental factors. Do the existing plants cast shade over the areas to be replanted? Are they likely to spread out rapidly again? If they are, anything new will have to be vigorous enough to compete and to look after itself.

This common garden problem is looked at in more detail in the chapter on New Life for Old Borders.

Features to be Hidden or Removed

Gardens often contain items that are essential but unattractive; examples might include sheds, fencing, large blank areas of house wall, compost bins, vegetable gardens and a garage or car port. Usually, these features look even worse when they belong to next door rather than to yourself. Sometimes the entire prospect from a garden is undesirable – you may, for instance, look out over an industrial site.

Hiding such eyesores as quickly and completely as possible is generally what is required, and this usually means using fast-growing evergreens. Hedges or screening trees or shrubs can be planted to hide unattractive views or large structures beyond the garden boundary. The temptation to make use of the extremely rapid-growing leyland cypress (× *Cupressocyparis leylandii*) should be resisted. Its aggressive growth sucks moisture and nutrients from the surrounding soil, and it can easily get completely out of hand.

An alternative to screening is to use a trellis with climbers. Most, including honeysuckles (*Lonicera* spp.) and clematis, are quite fast growing and often produce very attractive flowers. Although very few are evergreen, the thick, twiggy growth of established climbers still acts as a winter screen.

If you do establish a screening planting, consider how it can be made more attractive by growing something really dramatic in front of it. Remember, too, that hedges can frequently make good backdrops for flowers or coloured foliage, especially the dark green foliage of yew (*Taxus baccata*).

The thought of a hedge, a wall of dark green, may be rather depressing, but try thinking creatively – nearly all shrubs (or even trees, for that matter) can potentially be made into hedges. If you can buy them cheaply enough or perhaps even propagate them yourself, why not use flowering shrubs, either on their own or interspersed with more conventional hedging plants? You could even use trees with dramatic autumn colour; I wanted some more autumn shades in my own garden but did not have enough space left for any more trees, so I included some American oaks (bought very cheaply as damaged stock) in a hedge.

If you need to plant a screening hedge, how wide and tall will it have to be? Remember that hedges can get quite thick, which may impinge on the garden. If this may be a problem, consider a trellis with climbers which do not take up so much sideways space. Or concentrate on looking for upright-growing shrubs, which also take little sideways space, or think about bamboos.

How quickly do you want to create a screen? If you are impatient, your options will be more limited and probably less attractive.

How high do you want the screen to be? If it does not have to be too high, try to select screening shrubs that do not grow tall – you will only waste time clipping them to size.

Do you need to cover the top of an object as well as the sides? If this is the case, trellis that reaches over the top should be considered, with climbers that can go up and over.

Turn to the chapter on 'Instant' Gardens for more ideas on rapid-growing plants for screening.

Undervalued Features and Aspects

What are the good things about your garden? Are you sure that they are seen to best advantage? All too often, shrubs that are really too big for the spaces where they are put end up blocking good views, and ornaments are hidden and attractive plants concealed, simply because someone, not so many years ago, got carried away at the garden centre and bought a few attractive little flowering shrubs and did not look at the labels to see how big they would get.

In circumstances such as these it pays to be ruthless. By all means take time over making a decision, but do not be afraid of hacking down plants that get in the way. You will almost certainly be pleasantly surprised by the improvement in the view and the increased light and space. If this seems too drastic, it is possible to cut shrubs

down to ground level, allowing them the option of sprouting back next year (which most are capable of doing with a vengeance). If you do decide to get rid of them altogether, you will have to remove the stump to prevent regrowth.

Views are the most obvious lost opportunities in the garden. They could be views of far distant scenery or of an attractive neighbouring garden. But what about views within the garden? Are there attractive features that really deserve to be better seen? Or places that could be made to look more attractive and to be shown off to advantage?

A key part of making the best of views is to point them out to people by framing them or by creating a vista, whereby surrounding planting directs the eye onward. But take care that whatever makes up the framework is not so eye-catching that it draws attention away from what it is trying to frame! Simple shapes are more effective than complex planting and greenery is more useful than colour in this respect. Tall, narrow cypresses (*Cupressus* spp.) or clipped yews (*Taxus* spp.) or box (*Buxus* spp.) are traditional and highly effective. Perhaps the ultimate framework planting is a 'window' cut into an existing hedge.

Ground-cover or other low-growing plants can also be used as a foreground for a view, or, on a smaller scale, to surround something like a garden ornament or in front of a summerhouse. Such planting should be attractive but subtle – foliage plants or flowers with pastel shades would work well, for example.

Have you chosen the right plant? Framework planting needs to be quite precise. There is no point in planting something that is going to spread out and hide whatever it is you want to enhance.

What are the optimum dimensions you hope to achieve? Will what you choose look good all year round, including through the winter? Is it subtle enough not to detract from the view or feature?

Colour

Colour is the main source of pleasure that most gardeners derive from plants. It is also a source of much dissension. Colour arouses strong emotions, and feelings about it are deeply personal. It is important that you do what you feel happy with rather than what you think is fashionable. A garden planted from the heart is going to be more successful and give you more pleasure than one planted with a determination to 'get it right'. If you like shocking people, you will have plenty of scope.

There is no doubt that effective colour combinations are one of the best ways of transforming your garden. In this section we look at easy ways to do this by creating harmonious colour combinations and at how to improve and add to existing plantings. Finally, we take a closer look at the use of coloured foliage as an alternative to relying on flower colour.

Colour Schemes

The most effective way of using colour is to think in terms of colour schemes. This is an easy way of creating impact and creating an illusion of highly sophisticated planning.

ONE-COLOUR PLANTINGS

The discipline of planting a border with only one colour is a neat way of creating real impact, and one that, provided you can restrict yourself in your plant buying, is fun.

White gardens or borders have enjoyed a vogue for some time, perhaps because there are simply so many good plants with white flowers – nearly all popular flowering varieties have white forms, although many of these are,

Above: White gardens are cool and refreshing. White flowers look particularly good alongside silver foliage, such as that of the tree used here – *Pyrus salicifolia*.

strictly speaking, cream or ivory rather than white. White- or silver-variegated foliage is often included, too. White gardens are cool and refreshing, and they work well at all times of year.

Single-colour yellow or pink borders give plenty of scope, too, although it helps to create some variation by including just a few plants of another colour – blue goes well with both yellow and pink, for example, and white always looks good with pink. The variation between different yellows and pinks is considerable, ranging from pale, subtle primroses and blush pinks to acid yellows and magentas. Pale yellow to yellow-green plantings are also easy, unusual and please most eyes. Different yellows work well together, too, but this is not necessarily true with pinks. The stronger pinks tend to 'elbow' their way to the front of the border, making the paler shades look washed out. The moral with pink is to know it before you buy it. Plants with yellow-tinged foliage can be included in yellow borders, or, if you want a bit of contrast, try something with purple- or bronze-coloured foliage. Silver or grey foliage looks especially effective with pink flowers.

Blue borders are more difficult, partly because nearly all blue flowers are, in fact, mauve-purple-violet rather than pure blue, and the variation in colour tones is very wide. Yellow foliage works very well with blue flowers.

Red borders can be dark, almost depressing, because red is a very dark colour – notice how it is the first flower colour to disappear at dusk.

TWO- AND THREE-COLOUR PLANTINGS

The rule here must be to choose two colours you like together. They could be 'safe' and popular options, such as blue-mauve and yellow, or pink and blue, or pink and silver (foliage). Red and yellow contrast more strongly, or you could use traditional combinations, like red and white or blue-mauve and white. You might even want to try 'shocking' combinations that will provoke comment, like dark purple and silver or orange and deep pink-magenta. Such two-colour combinations make a strong impact.

Paradoxically, strong combinations work more easily (or cause fewer people to look away in horror) at dull times of year, like spring or autumn, or in very bright sunlight in Mediterranean or subtropical climates. This is because at times when the light level is very low, only the strong colours really stand out, and when they are very high, paler colours appear bleached. Dull summer skies, however, allow the subtlety of paler combinations to be appreciated, which is why pastel-shaded borders are so successful in many cooler temperate regions.

A scheme restricted to two colour groups allows you to create a powerful effect. Here deep mauve *Primula drummondii* grows alongside yellow narcissi and blue *Brunnera macrophylla*.

Pastel colours are easy and rewarding to mix, but any yellows involved should be soft, like the *Sisyrinchium striatum* here, nicely complemented by *Geranium* x *magnificum*.

EASY COLOUR GROUPINGS

Using three or more colours but restricting your choice of varieties is more difficult, but is still easier than trying to balance the whole palette in a border. Colours fall into groups for good scientific reasons. 'Cool' colours, such as blues, greens, yellow-greens and pinks, work well together and have a relaxing effect. 'Hot' colours, such as reds, oranges and yellows, work well together, too, but they are psychologically more demanding.

PASTEL COLOUR SCHEMES

Pastel schemes are among the most popular of all arrangements. Not only do they look good under grey skies, but they are soothing and there is a vast amount of plant material that can be used. Pinks, blues, mauves and whites are blended with silver and grey foliage, usually with soft pink being the dominant or theme colour. Pastel schemes are firmly associated with what are seen as traditional English gardens. In actual fact, the 'tradition' is not even as old

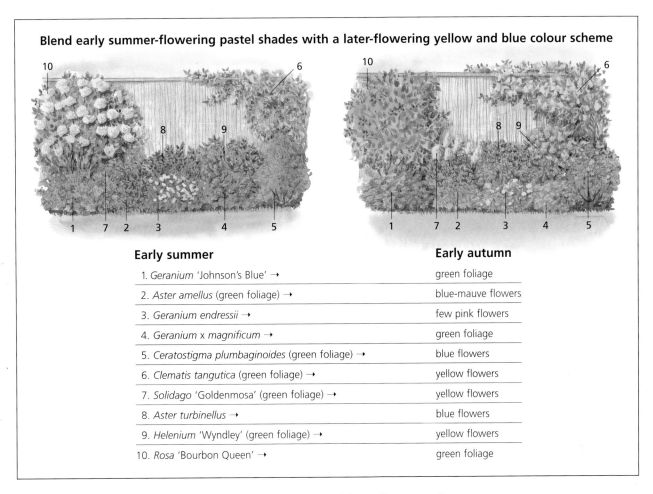

Blend early summer-flowering pastel shades with a later-flowering yellow and blue colour scheme

Early summer	Early autumn
1. *Geranium* 'Johnson's Blue' →	green foliage
2. *Aster amellus* (green foliage) →	blue-mauve flowers
3. *Geranium endressii* →	few pink flowers
4. *Geranium* x *magnificum* →	green foliage
5. *Ceratostigma plumbaginoides* (green foliage) →	blue flowers
6. *Clematis tangutica* (green foliage) →	yellow flowers
7. *Solidago* 'Goldenmosa' (green foliage) →	yellow flowers
8. *Aster turbinellus* →	blue flowers
9. *Helenium* 'Wyndley' (green foliage) →	yellow flowers
10. *Rosa* 'Bourbon Queen' →	green foliage

as the twentieth century, much of the popularity of this kind of colour scheming dating back to the work of Gertrude Jekyll in the 1920s.

This is the classic colour scheme for early summer, for many of the best pastel-coloured plants flower at this time, the most important being the old-fashioned roses in their myriad shades of pink, along with many varieties of hardy geranium. Phlox can be used to keep the scheme running into midsummer, but after this it is not easy to keep it going for much longer. Consider having another colour scheme for late summer and autumn – yellow daises, such as sunflowers and rudbeckia, and blue-mauve asters, for example. The plants for this scheme can be intermingled with the earlier-flowering pastel ones.

As well as silver foliage, plants with silver or cream variegation consort well with pastel colour schemes, especially where a lot of dark or strong pinks are used. Many people find such shades a bit oppressive used together; the flashes of silver provide some much needed light relief.

HOT COLOUR SCHEMES

Red, yellow and orange combinations, with their associations with sunny, tropical or Mediterranean climates, are wonderful for conveying a feeling of exoticism or of confidence in your planting style. They do rely on a more restricted range of varieties than pastel schemes, with many of the best oranges and reds, such as dahlias and cannas, being half-hardy. A hot planting will tend to look at its best towards the end of the summer and on into the early autumn, when the range of flowers in these colours will be at its widest.

As an alternative to using half-hardy plants for the rich oranges that seem so rare among reliably frost-hardy ones, annuals can be used instead. Many annuals – marigolds (both the *Tagetes* and *Calendula* kinds), Californian poppies (*Eschscholzia* spp.) and zinnias and nasturtiums (*Tropaeoleum* spp.), for example – have good orange flowers. These will all be relatively low growing and at their best in the latter part of the season.

Hot colours are particularly successful in late summer and mix well with dark foliage.
Dahlia 'Bishop of Llandaff' is not hardy and will need to be protected over winter.

There will be no shortage of yellow, especially in the last few months of the growing season, when there are so many – mostly quite large – yellow members of the daisy family in flower – sunflowers (*Helianthus* spp.), sneezeweed (*Helenium* spp.), rudbeckia, golden rod (*Solidago* spp.) and (a usefully low-growing one) tickseed (*Coreopsis* spp.).

Coloured foliage will be invaluable for combining with hot colours. Yellow-leaved shrubs, such as *Physocarpus opulifolius* 'Dart's Gold', grasses, or even some red- and purple-leaved plants can also be used, although bear in mind that the overall effect of too much dark foliage with red flowers can be depressing.

Creating Colour Schemes Without Wholesale Replanting

The thought of creating a colour-schemed garden or border may be alluring – think of all that praise from your friends for being 'so artistic', not to mention the pleasure it brings – but might it not involve replanting the whole garden? Not necessarily; in fact, it may mean refining what

exists already. If it is your own garden, you may subconsciously have chosen plants that are compatible anyway.

Go and take a look around or study photographs you have taken if it is winter time. What are the theme plants in the garden – that is, which ones dominate and set the tone? (With luck, the answer will not be nettles or Japanese knotweed). What colour are they? Is there a predominant colour or colour combination? If there is, could you make it the theme colour for the garden or a section of the planting? Of course, it may be that there is a different theme colour for different seasons.

Choosing a theme plant for a particular time of year in a border is a good way to simplify the planning process. Other plants can then be chosen to complement the theme plant, either picking up the same colour or providing a complementary one, which could be in harmony or contrasting. If there is already a good theme plant, you may only have to buy a few other new ones to create a striking impression. It is often possible to transform a border by taking out a few plants and propagating from the best of those already there.

It may well be necessary to remove plants if they do not conform to the new scheme. Small shrubs can often be lifted without damage and used elsewhere in the garden or given away, while perennials can be divided and also given away or donated to one of the increasing number of charitable plant sales. Often the removal of only a few plants and replacement with others will make a dramatic difference.

When you are choosing new plants for the scheme it is important that you are absolutely sure about the colour. Photographs in books are not always reliable, especially where blue is concerned. A garden notebook is a great help for recording your impressions of plants and you can refer to it later on.

Selecting Plants for Colour

If there are no obvious theme plants already for a particular season, it might be an idea to choose some, because it is the theme plants that really have the ability to transform a garden.

A theme plant for spring could be a large shrub with colourful flowers, such as a forsythia or viburnum, with bulbs or early perennials to complement it. Alternatively, it could be a reliably long-lived bulb, such as a yellow daffodil, which is widely planted in small clumps. A summer theme plant could be a flowering shrub, such as a rose, or a shrub with coloured foliage, but it is more likely to be a perennial, such as a hardy geranium or aster. Autumn theme plants are most likely to be perennials or perhaps

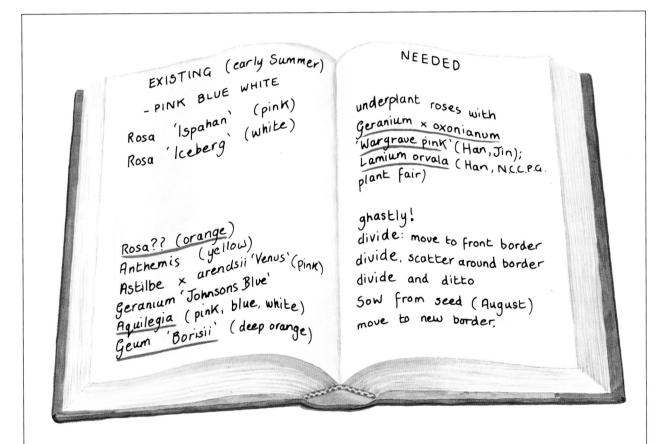

Use a garden notebook when you are re-planning a border. The left-hand side lists what is currently there. It has been decided to make the aquilegias the theme plant (underlined in red) in a pink-blue-white scheme and to remove those plants underlined in green. On the right-hand side the action to be taken is noted, with the plants that are to be propagated or bought (underlined in blue and followed by an abbreviation of possible sources) to produce a more consistent colour scheme.

There is nothing quite like silver and grey foliage to liven up a garden. This is *Cynara cardunculus*, with *Stachys byzantina* in front.

a small tree or shrub with outstanding berries. While only one specimen of a shrub will be needed to set the theme for a planting, if you rely on perennials or bulbs it will be necessary to have several, scattered around in places where they will be highly visible.

The value of theme plants with coloured foliage cannot be overestimated. They have a long season of interest and often make an extremely effective foil for the stronger and more concentrated colours of flowers. *Robinia pseudoacacia* 'Frisia', a small tree with divided, green-yellow leaves, is a wonderful complement to blue and violet flowers, for example.

It is not necessary to have only one theme plant for a particular season, but it is vital that, if there is more than one, they work together well. For example, in a border in my own garden, I use a powerful combination of a dark red thistle and a clear blue hardy geranium for early to midsummer. All the other colours should relate to the theme colours – blues, pinks and creamy-whites.

Livening up the Garden with Coloured Foliage

More and more gardeners appreciate foliage as a source of colour in the garden, a fact now recognized by the nursery industry, which seems to have decided that this is such an important area that one could be excused for thinking that it is essential for a plant to have coloured foliage before it is launched onto the market. As a result, recent years have seen a great increase in the number of plant varieties with leaves in shades other than green, including gold and silver variegated, and yellow, purple and bronze flushed. Many of these are evergreens, which makes them even more valuable.

SILVER AND GREY FOLIAGE

Plants with leaves in shades of silver, grey or blue-grey are often native to dry environments; the colour results from the presence of tiny light-reflecting hairs on the leaves, which serve to reduce the amount of moisture lost from the leaf surface. Consequently, plants such as lavenders (*Lavandula* spp.), santolina and common sage (*Salvia officinalis*) are very useful for dry areas. Nearly all are evergreen, too, which means that they are doubly useful. A few silver plants dotted around a border help to provide some flashes of light through dark winter days when everything else has died back or lost its leaves.

Many of the popular silver- or grey-leaved plants are dwarf or low-growing shrubs, whose bushy habit is a good counterpoint to erect perennials or much larger shrubs. Silver grasses are another important and useful group – the tiny *Festuca ovina* is a lovely blue-grey and looks good when it is grown in groups intermingled with heathers with darker foliage. The larger *Elymus magellanicus* has perhaps the finest blue-grey foliage of all.

As with silver- and white-variegated foliage (see page 38), silver- or grey-leaved plants are useful components of pastel colour schemes, but they are less successful with yellow flowers or golden-leaved plants. Unlike variegated plants, which are easily overdone, silver-leaved plants look good together, which is perhaps not surprising since many grow alongside each other naturally. Indeed, a good planting scheme for a hot, dry bank would be a mass of grey and silver plants, subtly contrasting their different tones and making the most of the great differentiation in their foliage shapes. Try a combination of fine-leaved grasses, clumpy lavenders and dramatic architectural thistles, such as the cotton thistle (*Onopordum acanthium*).

GOLDEN OR YELLOW FOLIAGE

Some plants naturally have golden- or yellow-flushed foliage, notably certain grasses and related plants, such as some of the New Zealand sedges, including *Carex testacea*. Unknown outside the ranks of connoisseurs a few

Blue and yellow go well together. Blue-leaved *Hosta sieboldiana* is surrounded by yellow foliage, including the grass *Milium effusum* 'Aureum'.

years ago, these are especially welcome recruits to the garden centre, for they are adaptable and reliable as well as being cheerfully evergreen.

The vast majority of plants with golden foliage are – like those with variegated leaves – the result of chance mutations, seized upon and then propagated by gardeners as novelties. Whether one likes them or not is purely and simply a matter of personal taste. As far as I am concerned there is little to choose between *Choisya ternata* 'Sundance', with its yellow-green foliage, and a rhododendron with a bad dose of chlorosis, the iron deficiency (the plant equivalent of anaemia) it will develop if grown on a lime-rich soil.

Such qualifications aside, there is no denying the usefulness of such plants in the garden, especially during the winter months, when anything yellow is to be welcomed as a reminder of sunshine and of summer. Some flourish in light shade, where their colour is greatly appreciated; the golden *Philadelphus coronarius* 'Aureus' is one excellent example, and the grass *Milium effusum* 'Aureum' is another.

Golden-yellow plants cannot be placed with the same carefree abandon as silver- and grey-leaved plants, for the simple reason that yellow is often a difficult colour to place in the border. The section on golden variegation (see page 38) looks at this problem in more detail.

Coloured foliage plants have a long season and can be used effectively together, although regular clipping may be necessary to prevent the more vigorous varieties from swamping others.

Red-, Purple- and Bronze-coloured Foliage

There are currently many fewer plant varieties with foliage in the red, purple and bronze range than with golden-yellow foliage, but nurseries are becoming increasingly aware of a growing public interest and new introductions are becoming more frequent. As with yellow-leaved plants, a minority of these occur naturally – the eye-catching, scarlet-tinged grass *Imperator cylindrica* 'Rubra', for example – with the majority being variants of green-leaved species. There are shrubs, like the well-known and reliable smoke bush (*Cotinus coggyria* 'Royal Purple'), perennials and several annuals, including a basil (*Ocimum basilicum* var. *purpurascens*). There are also a number of varieties with brown foliage, although in some cases it can be difficult to tell whether the plant is dead or alive.

Plants with red- or purple-tinged foliage are very useful for providing a counterpoint to the prevailing green, and given that they stand out more from their fellows than do golden-leaved varieties, they are ideal for interval planting, to build up a sense of rhythm in a border. Again, unlike golden-leaved varieties, these plants work well with practically any other foliage or flower colours. The range of purple-leaved annuals is, of course, invaluable for adding spice to summer container plantings, hanging baskets and bedding displays.

Perhaps the most adventurous way to plant with dark-leaved forms is to combine them with golden and yellow foliage, with variegated varieties, including silver-variegated foliage. The fact that there are fewer purple-toned plants available does not necessarily matter, because only a few of them are necessary in a planting to provide variation within the dominant paler theme. Too many darker-leaved plants will look pretty dreary, anyway. Plantings like this, which rely for most of their impact on coloured foliage, provide interest over a long season.

Variegated Foliage

Variegation is in nearly all cases not 'naturally' occurring but the result of a chance mutation on which the horticulturist has seized; in the wild it would soon die out. Perhaps its inherent 'unnaturalness' is why variegation arouses strong feelings among gardeners: many people seem drawn to it, some collect rare variegated forms with an enthusiasm bordering on fanaticism, but others quite openly hate it. There are some variegated plants that I adore; there are, however, others that I strongly dislike, and in this latter category are those spotty varieties that look as if they are diseased.

There is no doubt that variegated plants are one of the easiest ways to transform a garden. Their long season of interest – especially when they are evergreen – and their ability to bring light into dark areas of a garden can be invaluable. However, like wine, and certain of the other pleasures of life, they are to be taken in moderation. Too many different types of variegated plant can make a garden seem very 'fussy' and overstimulating, especially if they are placed next to each other. Much as I dislike gardening rules, one that is worth bearing in mind is: 'never put two variegated plants next to each other.'

Two other caveats need to be observed. The first is that, although variegated foliage is immensely useful for lightening shade, placing variegated plants in too dark a spot puts them under stress, because the leaves, lacking the

The brownish-purple-leaved *Heuchera micrantha* var. *diversifolia* 'Palace Purple', planted at intervals along the front of a border, is very effective at creating a sense of rhythm.

chemical chlorophyll that is essential for their physiology, tend to turn green. The only way to avoid leaving them to their fate in such places is to use them in containers, so that they can be moved – exchanged with one another, perhaps – and placed in the sun every few months.

The second point to consider is how unstable variegation is. Because it is, by its very nature, inefficient, shoots often 'revert', growing green leaves instead, which then grow more vigorously. If these all-green shoots are not ruthlessly cut out, they will eventually take over entirely, and species that are allowed to revert vary greatly from the variegated form.

Although the factors that cause variegation are numerous and complex, the end result for the gardener is that there are two clear categories: silver-white-cream variegation and gold-yellow variegation. We have already noted some of the uses of both groups.

Silver-white variegation, which is regarded as 'cool', works well with paler pastel colour schemes, contributing to the overall soothing harmony of the planting design. However, it is also useful for providing contrasts with stronger and brighter colours, acting as both a counterpoint and a calming influence. For example, the white-streaked grass *Glyceria maxima* var. *variegata* planted next to magenta loosestrife (*Lythrum salicaria*) is a pleasing combination to most eyes. This is why silver-white variegated plants are popular in summer container plantings, where many strongly coloured plants are brought together – the variegated form of *Felicia amelloides*, for example, will help to cool down bright pink petunias, scarlet salvias and ultramarine lobelia.

Gold-yellow variegation is another matter altogether, however. For a start, yellow and pink is an unpopular combination, yet how many of the new varieties of gold-variegated plants have pink flowers? The answer, I think, is far too many. This factor alone makes bringing golden plants into pastel schemes, which are usually strongly pink based, very problematic. Gold next to silver-grey foliage is often unsuccessful too, because silver looks greyer and muddier next to gold, an effect that also limits the use of yellow-flushed foliage plants. Combinations with blue-purple or with hot colours are much more successful.

PRACTICAL COLOUR SCHEMES FOR DIFFERENT TIMES OF YEAR

Spring – blue and yellow (useful for sun or light shade)

BLUES

bulbs:	species and cultivars of *Chionodoxa*, *Hyacinthoides*, *Muscari* and *Scilla*
perennials:	species and cultivars of *Ajuga*, *Omphalodes* and *Pulmonaria* (e.g. *P. longifolia* varieties); *Symphytum caucasicum*

YELLOWS

bulbs:	species and cultivars of *Narcissus* and *Tulipa* (yellow varieties)
perennials:	*Doronicum* (species); *Primula veris* (cowslip), *P. vulgaris* (primrose)
shrubs/climbers:	*Forsythia* (cultivars); *Jasminum officinale*

YELLOW-GREENS

shrubs:	*Euphorbia* (e.g., *E. amygdaloides* var. *robbiae*, *E. characias*, *E. polychroma*)

Early to midsummer – pink and pastel

PINKS

perennials:	species and cultivars of *Astilbe* and *Dicentra*; *Geranium* (especially *G. endressii* varieties); *Paeonia* (pink cultivars); *Persicaria bistorta* 'Superba'; *Stachys macrantha*; *Thalictrum* species
shrubs:	*Escallonia* 'Apple Blossom'; *Kalmia latifolia*; *Kolkwitzia amabilis*; *Lavatera* 'Rosea'; *Rosa* (roses; especially old-fashioned and shrubs varieties); *Syringa* (lilac; pink varieties)

BLUE-MAUVES

perennials: *Campanula* (species and cultivars); *Geranium* (e.g. *G.* 'Johnson's Blue', *G.* x *magnificum*); *Iris ensata* (cultivars), *I. sibirica*; *Nepeta* (species and cultivars); *Salvia nemorosa* (cultivars)

shrubs: *Abutilon vitifolium*; *Ceanothus*; *Lavandula*; *Rosmarinus officinalis*; *Syringa* (lilac varieties)

WHITES

bulbs: *Lilium candidum, L. regale*

perennials: *Achillea ptarmica*; *Astilbe* (white varieties); *Crambe* (species); *Dicentra* (white varieties); *Dictamnus albus*; *Gypsophila paniculata*; *Papaver orientale* and *Thalictrum* (white varieties)

shrubs: *Cistus* (white varieties); *Deutzia* (species and varieties); *Exochorda* x *macrantha* 'The Bride'; *Rosa* (white varieties); *Rubus* 'Benenden' (syn. *R.* Tridel 'Benenden'); *Spiraea nipponica* 'Snowmound'

SILVER-GREY FOLIAGE

perennials: *Anthemis punctata* subsp. *cupaniana*; *Artemisia alba* 'Canescens', *A. ludoviciana*; *Lamium* (silver cultivars,); *Stachys byzantina*

grasses: *Elymus magellanicus*; *Festuca glauca* (and cultivars); *Helictotrichon sempervirens*

shrubs (dwarf): *Artemisia* (species); *Convolvulus cneorum*; *Lavandula* (species); *Lotus hirsutus*; *Ruta graveolens*; *Santolina chamaecyparissus*

Late summer to early autumn – blue and yellow

BLUE-MAUVES

perennials: cultivars of *Aster amellus*, *A.* x *frikartii*, *A. novae-angliae*, *A. novi-belgii*; *Felicia amelloides* (tender); *Liriope muscari*; *Perovskia atriplicifolia*; *Salvia patens* (tender); *Vernonia* (species)

shrubs: species and cultivars of *Caryopteris* and *Ceratostigma*; some *Ceanothus* (e.g. *C.* 'Autumnal Blue')

YELLOWS

perennials: *Chrysanthemum* (species and cultivars); *Crocosmia* (some); *Helianthus*; *Helenium*; *Rudbeckia*; *Solidago*; x *Solidaster*

climbers: *Clematis orientalis, C. tangutica*

HOT COLOURS

Oranges

annuals: *Eschscholzia californica*; *Tithonia rotundifolia*; *Tropaeolum majus*

perennials: *Crocosmia* (many cultivars); *Canna* (tender; many cultivars); *Dahlia* (tender; many cultivars); *Helenium* (some cultivars); *Physalis alkekengi* (fruit)

REDS

annuals: *Zinnia* (cultivars)

perennials: *Canna* (tender; many cultivars); *Dahlia* (tender; many cultivars, especially *D.* 'Bishop of Llandaff'); *Penstemon barbatus*; *Phygelius capensis*; *Salvia* (especially *S. elegans* 'Scarlet Pineapple'/ syn. *S. rutilans*, *S. fulgens*, *S. microphylla*, all tender); *Schizostylis coccinea*; *Tropaeolum speciosum* (climbing); *Zauschneria californica*

PURPLE FOLIAGE

annuals: *Atriplex hortensis* var. *rubra*; *Beta vulgaris* 'Bull's Blood' and varieties sold as the vegetable ruby chard; *Ocimum basilicum* var. *purpurascens*; *Perilla frutescens* var. *rubra*; *Ricinus communis*

perennials: *Heuchera micrantha* var. *diversifolia* 'Palace Purple'; *Lysimachia ciliata* 'Firecracker'; *Sedum telephium* subsp. *maximum* 'Atropurpureum'

shrubs: *Berberis thunbergii* f. *atropurpurea*; *Cotinus coggygria* 'Royal Purple'; *Sambucus nigra* 'Guincho Purple'

Improving an Existing Colour Scheme

The illustration on the left shows a border containing well-established shrubs, several of which have seen better days, together with some rather congested perennials. Only a rough plan need be made, with a scale to keep track of relative plant spreads. Draw the outlines of the plants and fill them in with the appropriate colours for one particular time of year (the illustrations cover early to midsummer). Note the good and bad points. The illustration on the right shows the improved colour scheme.

Good

• The purple cotinus and silver senecio are in good shape and look good together.

• The hypericum and berberis work well together.

Bad

• The lavatera is old and in bad shape; its dark pink looks awful next to the silver senecio. Likewise the cistus, which is well shaped but, as you know, short lived.

• The tellima and alchemilla dominate the front with a mass of greenery but little colour.

• The spiraea is spectacular when in flower but otherwise dull.

• There is very little interest later in the year.

What is needed

• A scheme based on a theme colour of dark purple foliage (the existing cotinus and berberis). The silver of the senecio is a good long-season foliage contrast . Concentrate on adding red-purple and blue-mauve tones, which will go well with the theme colour and with the yellow-flowered shrubs.

• Some later season colour.

Action

• Remove the awkward yellow-pink clash by taking out the lavatera and cistus (neither is a long-lived shrub anyway).

• Thin the tellima and alchemilla by about two-thirds.

• Add a selection of later flowering perennials with either deep pink-red-purple or blue-mauve flowers.

• Add a *Rubus thibetanus*, which has prominent white stems in the winter.

• Encourage a late-flowering clematis to scramble through and over the spiraea.

1. *Cotinus coggygria* 'Royal Purple'

2. *Cistus creticus*

3. *Brachyglottis* (Dunedin Group) 'Sunshine' (syn. *Senecio* 'Sunshine')

4. *Lavatera* 'Rosea'

5. *Hypericum* 'Hidcote'

6. *Berberis thunbergii* f. *atropurpurea*

7. *Iris sibirica*

8. *Tellima grandiflora*

9. *Alchemilla mollis*

10. *Spiraea* x *vanhouttei*

11. *Aster* x *frikartii* 'Mönch' (midsummer to autumn)

12. *Rubus thibetanus* (winter)

13. *Eupatorium purpureum* subsp. *maculatum* 'Atropurpureum' (late summer)

14. *Aster novae-angliae* 'Septemberrubin' (autumn)

15. *Clematis* 'Madame Julia Correvon' (mid- to late summer)

16. *Heuchera micrantha* var. *diversifolia* 'Palace Purple'

17. *Geranium wallichianum* 'Buxton's Variety' (autumn)

18. *Knautia macedonica* (midsummer)

19. *Monarda* 'Capricorn' (midsummer)

Bright Flowers for Impact

These are just a few of the plants that can really stop the traffic with their flowers. In borders they need careful placing because they demand instant attention.

Fremontodendron californicum

Fremontodendron californicum

- Evergreen shrub/small tree
- 3 x 2m (10 x 6ft), potentially 5m (16ft) in sheltered sites
- Like rays of sunshine, large yellow flowers adorn this grey-leaved Californian shrub through summer and autumn.
- Full sun, good drainage and shelter from winds are vital. Thrives on chalk and builder's rubble – an ideal wall shrub.

Geranium psilostemon

- Clump-forming herbaceous perennial
- 80 x 80cm (32 x 32in)
- Dark-eyed, purple-magenta flowers, borne in early to midsummer, look wonderful next to soft blue *Veronica longifolia*, pale green euphorbias or grey *Lysimachia ephemerum*.
- An easy, vigorous species for full sun or light shade on any reasonable soil. The hybrid *G.* 'Patricia' is very similar but half the size.

Lychnis coronaria

(rose campion, dusty miller)

- Short-lived herbaceous perennial
- 70 x 30cm (28 x 12in)
- Magenta-cerise flowers, which can be seen a mile off, and a self-seeding habit make this a classic cottage-garden plant. The clumps of grey, felty leaves are attractive, too. Looks good with blues.
- Grow in any reasonable soil in sun.

Lythrum salicaria

(purple loosestrife)

- Erect-growing herbaceous perennial
- 110 x 50cm (43 x 20in)
- Magenta-pink flowers in tight spikes, freely produced from mid-to late summer, make this a valuable perennial for borders or wild gardens in full sun. Naturally a wetland plant, it thrives anywhere that does not dry out. Grey-leaved macleaya, pink filipendulas and lilac monardas seem natural colour and habitat companions.
- Note: Although it does not self-seed notably in the garden, it can be a serious nuisance in wetland areas where it is not native, such as in North America.

Tropaeolum speciosum

(flame creeper, Scottish flame flower)

- Herbaceous climber
- 3 x 0.5m (10ft x 20in)
- A member of the nasturtium family, with brilliant scarlet flowers and blue berries, it does best in mild and moist areas. Often grown up yew hedges, where its flowers stand out against the dark green in late summer and autumn.
- Light shade and well-drained soil that never dries out essential.

Further suggestions

Yellow – *Caltha palustris* (marsh marigold, kingcup); *Eranthis hyemalis* (syn. *Aconitum hyemale*; winter aconite); *Forsythia* spp.; *Trollius europaeus* (common globeflower)

Orange – *Alstroemeria aurea* (syn. *A. aurantiaca*); *Asclepias tuberosa* (butterfly weed); *Calendula officinalis* (pot marigold); *Fritillaria imperialis* (crown imperial)

Red – *Crocosmia* 'Lucifer'; *Dahlia* 'Bishop of Llandaff', *Lobelia cardinalis* (cardinal flower); *Monarda* 'Squaw'; *Rosa* 'Geranium' (*R. moyesii* hybrid); *Salvia fulgens* (syn. *S. cardinalis*)

Pink – *Bergenia* 'Abendglut', *B. purpurascens* (syn. *B. beesiana*), *B.* 'Sunningdale'; *Geranium sanguineum*, *G.* x *riversleaianum* 'Russell Prichard'; *Rosa* 'Zéphirine Drouhin'

Pastel Colours you Cannot go Wrong With

The following plants are available in some of the best restful pastel shades. They are easy to combine with other pastels, or with darker blues, violets, pinks and reds.

Geranium endressii

• Semi-evergreen, clump-forming herbaceous perennial

• 40 x 60cm (16 x 24in)

• This species and its hybrids and associated species are incredibly useful garden plants – as underplanting for roses and other shrubs, as weed-suppressing wild garden plants and as early-season 'fillers' among taller, later flowering border perennials like asters. *G. versicolor* has palest pink flowers, attractively veined in deeper pink; *G.* x *oxonianum* 'Wargrave Pink' has salmon flowers; the flowers of *G. endressii* itself can vary from the softest pink to an aggressive magenta; *G.* x *oxonianum* 'Claridge Druce' has strong pink flowers and is a first-class weed crusher. All flower profusely in early summer, with more flushes of bloom until late autumn.

• Plant in sun or shade in all soils except for the very poorest and driest.

Geranium pratense

'Mrs Kendall Clark'

• Erect-growing herbaceous perennial

• 80 x 60cm (32 x 24in)

• The lavender-blue flowers have prominent white veining. This is a beautiful and subtle plant, flowering in midsummer, which looks good with strong pinks, such as *Lythrum salicaria*.

• Plant in any soil, including wet ones, in full sun.

Penstemon

'Apple Blossom'

• Herbaceous perennial

• 70 x 60cm (28 x 24in)

• Spikes of beautifully soft pink, tubular flowers capture that two-tone pink that is so characteristic of apple blossom. This plant flowers from midsummer well into autumn and looks good with grey foliage and other penstemon varieties. It is not hardy in very cold areas and, like all penstemons, is irritatingly short lived. It is easy to propagate from cuttings, though.

• Plant in full sun and well-drained, fertile soil.

Perovskia atriplicifolia

• Erect-growing herbaceous perennial

• 100 x 60cm (36 x 24in)

• A haze of exquisite violet-blue flowers, borne in multi-stemmed spikes, makes this one of the most valuable midsummer perennials. Its skeleton of white-grey stems in winter and strongly aromatic leaves add to its value. It is a good companion for herbs and other aromatic plants, like lavender.

• Full sun and good drainage are essential, and the plant is good on dry and thin soils.

Veronica gentianoides

• Slowly spreading herbaceous perennial

• 30 x 40cm (12 x 16in)

• Spikes of powder-blue flowers in late spring are few and far between, so this is a plant to make the most of at the front of borders, alongside euphorbias, perhaps, or as a filler in gaps among later flowering perennials.

• Plant in full sun and in any soil that does not seriously dry out.

Further suggestions

Pinks – *Dianthus* spp.; *Diascia* spp.; *Dicentra spectabilis* (bleeding heart, Dutchman's breeches); *Digitalis* x *mertonensis*; *Magnolia* x *soulangeana*; *Malus floribunda*; *Phlox* spp.; *Rosa* spp.; *Sidalcea* spp.

Blues – *Agapanthus* spp.; *Aquilegia vulgaris* (columbine, granny's bonnet); *Camassia cusickii*; *Caryopteris* x *clandonensis*; *Ceratostigma* spp.; *Convolvulus sabatius* (syn. *C. mauritanicus*); *Geranium* 'Johnson's Blue'; *Lithodora diffusa* (syn. *Lithospermum diffusum*); *Nepeta* x *faassenii*; *Veronica austriaca*

Violets and lilacs – *Buddleja davidii* var. *nanhoensis*; *Clematis alpina*; *Hesperis matronalis* (sweet rocket, dame's violet); *Penstemon* 'Sour Grapes'; *Syringa* spp.; *Viola cornuta* (horned violet)

Good Whites

Most white flowers are actually off-white, like all those white paints that are really ultra-pale something else. This is a small selection of the most useful clean whites.

Epilobium angustifolium
'Album'

- Strongly spreading herbaceous perennial
- 1.2 x 1m (4 x 3ft)
- The pure white flowers in spikes illuminate the midsummer border. Surrounding dark foliage shows it at its best. Not as aggressively spreading as its infamous parent, the bright pink rosebay willowherb, but it is still one to watch.
- Grow in any reasonable soil in full sun.

Leucanthemella serotina
(syn. *Chrysanthemum serotinum*, *C. uliginosum*)

- Spreading herbaceous perennial
- 1.2 x 0.6m (4 x 2ft)
- The last really hardy perennial to flower before the gales and frosts of autumn force it, too, to retreat underground, this plant has lovely big, white daisies atop tall, erect stems. It looks great with asters.
- Plant in full sun and any reasonable soil. It can spread aggressively in damp ground.

Papaver orientale
'Black and White'

- Clump-forming herbaceous perennial
- 70 x 70cm (28 x 28in)
- A truly unique colour combination: white flowers with large black basal blotches. Flowering in early summer, it dies back by midsummer, so needs the companionship of other, later flowering perennials. It looks especially fine with red and orange poppies.
- Grow in full sun and well-drained soil.

Rubus
'Benenden'
(syn. *R*. Tridel 'Benenden')

- Deciduous shrub
- 2 x 2m (6 x 6ft)
- In early summer the large white flowers on this erect-growing shrub convince most onlookers that they are roses. Tolerating some shade, it is tailormade for filling boring gaps at the edges of tree canopies or placing in front of dark and dreary hedges. The adventurous could combine it with a late-flowering *Clematis viticella*.
- Plant in any reasonable soil.

Sorbus cashmiriana
(Kashmir rowan)

- Deciduous small tree
- 3m (10ft) after 10 years, 7 x 3m (23 x 10ft) ultimately
- White berries can be rather a surprise, and they seem to be less readily eaten by the birds, who leave them on the tree until well into the winter. There is attractive pinnate foliage, and cream flowers appear in spring.
- Plant in any reasonable soil in full sun.

Further suggestions

Agapanthus campanulatus var. *albidus*; *Amelanchier* spp. (serviceberry); *Argyranthemum foeniculaceum*; *Campanula persicifolia* 'Alba'; *Dictamnus albus* (burning bush); *Geranium clarkei* 'Kashmir White'; *Gypsophila paniculata* (baby's breath); *Libertia* spp.; *Lilium candidum* (Madonna lily); *L. regale* (regal lily); *Magnolia stellata* (star magnolia); *Malus hupehensis*; *Phlox paniculata* 'Fujiyama'; *Prunus* 'Taihaku'; *Rosa* 'Iceberg'; *Solanum jasminoides* 'Album'; *Spiraea* 'Arguta'

Unusual Colours

Unusual colours attract interest and add panache to plantings. Seeking out some of these less commonly seen plants can be a rewarding exercise.

Cosmos atrosanguineus
(chocolate cosmos)

- Herbaceous perennial
- 60 x 40cm (24 x 16in)
- Not only are the dark red flowers very unusual in shade, but their scent is of chocolate – so strong that it takes some effort of will not to take a bite. Flowering in late summer, the plant's half-hardiness means that it is usually grown in a container or as part of a summer bedding scheme. It should be taken under cover in winter.
- Plant in full sun and any reasonable soil.

Cosmos atrosanguineus

Symphytum caucasicum

Geranium phaeum
(dusky cranesbill)
- Slowly spreading, clump-forming herbaceous
  perennial
- 40 x 60cm (24 x 16in)
- Known as the 'mourning widow' for the sombre shade of its
  flowers, this robust cranesbill has numerous varieties, in shades of
  maroon, black-brown, pink and dark purple. All thrive in sun or
  light shade, and because they are the earliest geraniums to flower,
  they make a striking contrast with yellow-green euphorbias
  in late spring.
- Grow in any reasonable soil.

Knautia macedonica
- Clump-forming herbaceous perennial
- 60 x 60cm (24 x 24in)
- Are they red or pink? The flowers are one of those colours that is
  impossible to describe. A scabious with a dark colour that
  immediately attracts attention throughout midsummer, this plant
  combines well with blue-mauve flowers such as other scabious,
  perovskia and lavender.
- Full sun and good drainage are essential. Some drought will
  be tolerated.

Potentilla atrosanguinea var. atrosanguinea
- Clump-forming perennial
- 30 x 60cm (12 x 24in)
- Dark red flowers are characteristic of this midsummer-flowering
  perennial, which looks a bit like a silver-leaved strawberry plant
  until it flowers. Unfortunately, it flops terribly after flowering, so
  might need some disguising or hiding.
- Plant in full sun and any reasonable soil. Likes moisture.

Salvia verticillata
'Purple Rain'
- Clump-forming perennial
- 40 x 50cm (16 x 20in)
- Deep, dusky purple calyces are prominent for several weeks in
  late summer. This is a good front-of-the-border plant to mix with
  taller asters and grasses.
- Plant in full sun and any reasonable soil. Some drought will
  be tolerated.

Symphytum caucasicum
- Strongly spreading, clump-forming perennial
- 60 x 80cm (24 x 32in)
- This comfrey is unusual in that its flowers are so, so blue – and
  not many 'blue' flowers really are. It flowers for ages in late
  spring and thrives in out-of-the-way corners, fighting off
  competition from weeds through its rather invasive habit.
- Grow in sun or light shade in any reasonable soil.

Viola
'Molly Sanderson'
- Short-lived perennial
- 10 x 15cm (4 x 6in)
- These have to be the blackest of flowers – eye-catching wherever
  they are planted and a good accompaniment to spring bulbs.
- Grow in sun or light shade and in fertile soil. Propagation from
  cuttings is easy.

Colourful Foliage
Of the increasing number of plants with coloured
foliage that are available, the following are among
the best – for one thing, they have been thoroughly
tried and tested.

Cotinus coggygria
'Royal Purple'
- Deciduous shrub
- 4 x 4m (13 x 13ft)
- The best purple-leaved shrub, dark and richly coloured, is a
  wonderful background to silver foliage and to pink and blue
  flowers. Late summer sees pale brown, 'smoke-like' seedheads,
  and there is good autumn colour.
- Grow in full sun and any reasonable soil.

Elymus magellanicus

- Slowly clump-forming herbaceous grass
- 40 x 40cm (16 x 16in), flowerheads to 70cm (28in)
- The finest blue-silver leaved plant, and without the running tendencies of other elymus grasses. It is a first-rate 'punctuation mark' in borders, especially with pink and blue flowers.
- Plant in full sun and any reasonable soil. It is probably quite drought resistant.

Euphorbia dulcis
'Chameleon'

- Slowly clump-forming herbaceous perennial
- 30 x 40cm (12 x 16in)
- The dark brown-purple foliage looks its best in spring, but is perfectly respectable later. It is good with blue and yellow bulbs and for dotting around with other low perennials, such as geraniums.
- Grow in sun or light shade and any reasonable soil.

Physocarpus opulifolius
'Dart's Gold'

- Deciduous shrub
- 2.5 x 3m (8 x 10ft)
- Golden-yellow leaves are borne on a compact shrub, with the palest pink flowers in spring.
- Grow in sun and any reasonable soil, including dry soil, although it dislikes shallow, alkaline ones. Strong sun may cause scorching.

Robinia pseudoacacia
'Frisia'

- Deciduous small tree
- 6 x 4m (20 x 13ft) after 10 years, 11 x 6m (36 x 20ft) ultimately
- I am often sceptical about yellow foliage, but this is a very good one – that is, it doesn't look diseased, but is a clean green-yellow that goes well with blue and violet flowers when the foliage is young and combines attractively with darker leaved trees when it is older.
- Plant in sun and any reasonable, preferably fertile soil.

Cheerful Evergreens

Traditional dark evergreens can add to the dreariness of winter. These evergreens will help cheer you up.

Carex hachijoensis
'Evergold'

- Evergreen grass-like plant, non-spreading clumps
- 25 x 40cm (10 x 16in)
- Always neat, the tufts of fine golden leaves bring life to dull winter borders in shade.
- It will grow in any reasonable soil, but appreciates moisture.

Cortaderia selloana
'Aureolineata'

- Evergreen grass-like plant, slowly spreading clumps
- 1.75 x 1.5m (5ft 6in x 5ft)
- However rude I may be about pampas grass, I take it all back for this most attractive plant, whose golden leaves are quite subtle in tone, warming in winter and a good mixer with 'hot' colour schemes in summer.
- Grow in full sun and any reasonable soil.

Elaeagnus pungens
'Maculata'

- Evergreen shrub
- 1.2 x 1.2m (4 x 4ft) after 5 years, 4 x 4m (13 x 13ft) ultimately
- Gold-splashed leaves on a strongly growing shrub make this an invaluable plant where winter cheer is needed. Occasional shoots revert, and these should be removed as fast as possible. It can be grown as a standard.
- Grow in sun or light shade and any reasonable soil. It dislikes cold winter winds.

Ilex x altaclarensis
'Golden King'

- Evergreen small tree
- 2 x 1.5m (6 x 5ft) after 5 years, 5 x 4m (16 x 13ft) ultimately
- Regarded by many as the best variegated holly, 'Golden King' is also perhaps the most attractive golden evergreen, although it is a little slow growing. Dense growth make it a good subject for clipping to shape. The leaves are almost spineless. Despite the name, it is female and has red berries.
- Grow in sun or light shade in any reasonable soil.

Creating Interest
with architectural plants

Going out and taking black and white photographs of your garden when it is in full bloom may seem a slightly eccentric thing to do, but the results can be very revealing. When the garden is shorn of the colour that creates its immediate impact, it is possible to concentrate on the variety of plant forms and to begin to think about how to improve its visual structure. Does it look like one great, indistinct blur? If so, then there are too many amorphous plants with lots of small leaves. Do particular plants stand out because of their shape or distinctive foliage? These are the plants that give a garden structure.

'Architectural' plants is the name often now given to these species. They are invaluable in a garden, not only because they provide structure but also because their long season of interest generates a feeling of continuity. Many of the best are evergreen, and some are most effective in winter when the play of their branches can be appreciated. Some others have characteristic flower stems, which turn into distinctive seedheads that last well into winter.

Evergreens for Year-round Architecture

Many evergreens have a clear and distinct habit. Examples include numerous conifers, which can range in size from the tall but narrow Serbian spruce (*Picea omorika*), essentially an ultra-slender Christmas tree, to the multitude of popular dwarf species. Although the latter have been so grossly overplanted as to become a byword for unimaginative low-maintenance schemes, they should not be scorned. Used sparingly, they can be useful for introducing an architectural touch into many different kinds of planting; the very slow-growing, upright Irish juniper (*Juniperus communis* 'Hibernica'), for example, is a good alternative 'punctuation mark' to the more traditional

clipped box (*Buxus* spp.), and it is less work because it does not need to be clipped to shape.

Planting trees for architectural interest is obviously a long-term proposition, but those with an eye to the future should consider the many magnificent conifers that can make a major difference not just to our gardens but to the whole landscape. Notable among these are the cedars (*Cedrus* spp.), the pines (*Pinus* spp.) and the wellingtonia (*Sequoiadendron giganteum*).

Yew (*Taxus* spp.) and box are the two evergreens that have traditionally been used to provide structure in the garden, and the trees are clipped into geometrical shapes from a young age. Indeed, the classical garden tradition, as seen at its best in France, Italy, Spain and Portugal, is almost entirely about using clipped trees and shrubs, most of them evergreens, so that the garden becomes an exercise in sculptured geometric forms. The success of many twentieth-century gardens is based on just this kind of core structure, fleshed out with masses of exuberant planting.

Lushly planted gardens that look chaotic or dull when seen through the veil of black and white photography can be transformed by the inclusion of some clipped

An avenue of clipped box and trimmed hedges create a sense of order in even very informal gardens.

shrubs to provide the 'bones'. Smartly upright yews or box pyramids at regular intervals are all that is needed to give a basic backbone to a border. Going one stage further, a border can be provided with a frame in the form of low box hedging around the edges.

The ordinary yew (*Taxus baccata*) and box (*Buxus sempervirens*) will grow faster than is often thought if they are fed generously with well-rotted manure in autumn or a balanced feed in spring. Yew grows faster and larger, so is more suitable for hedging to waist height and higher

Low box (*Buxus* spp.) hedging is an effective and traditional way of framing borders and vegetable gardens. Box is a greedy plant, though, so make sure there is a gap of about 30cm (12in) between it and the planting position of anything else.

or for use as clipped specimens. The branches of Irish yew (*T. baccata* 'Fastigiata', syn. *T. b.* 'Hibernica') sweep upwards, so it is ideal for developing narrow shapes. To create really narrow pillars, wire can be used to tie in the branches, which also helps to stop snow damage, a problem that tends to afflict conifers with upswept branches.

The imaginative gardener might want to experiment with clipping a much wider range of shrubby evergreens – a dense, twiggy habit of growth and small leaves are the important prerequisites.

Architectural Key Plants

The most effective use of architectural plants is as 'key plants' – that is, those that instantly stand out because of their shape and the position in which they are placed. The clipped shrubs just mentioned have often been used in this role, but a more modern approach is to use spiky plants, such as the cordyline, which is commonly seen growing in an urn as the focal point of a garden. It is so distinctive and symmetrical that it practically creates a focal point wherever it is put.

Any really spiky-looking plant makes a good focal point, as do very narrow, vertical ones like the Italian cypress (*Cupressus sempervirens*). An upright-growing plant that soars above its neighbours is sure to attract attention. While the most favoured upright growers are evergreens, small deciduous trees with such a habit can also be used, although in the majority of cases the overall form these develop in time tends to be vase- rather than pencil-shaped.

As well as the small number of very tight columnar trees. several others have distinctive narrow shapes.

Serbian spruce (*Picea omorika*) is the best narrow Christmas tree shape.

This shape includes several popular small trees, such as the flowering cherry *Prunus* 'Amanogawa'.

This is the more common vase-shape, seen in such trees as *Prunus* 'Pandora' and *Malus tschonoskii*.

Right: *Cordyline australis* is a highly effective plant for creating and focusing interest.

Ornamental grasses are excellent plants for emphasizing form and textural qualities.
This *Stipa gigantea* is particularly useful as it is visually striking but has a 'see through' quality.

Small, vase-shaped small trees make excellent key plants for gardens if they are not hemmed in by any larger, conventionally shaped trees. Because the trunk is an important part of the overall effect, the tree will look even more striking if the surrounding planting is kept low – as little more than ground cover, in fact. Such trees are discussed further in the chapter on Specimen Plants.

Although perennials cannot provide a constant key element in the garden, they can be used to give a strong sense of structure. Those with tall, spire-shaped flowerheads can be used to great effect, soaring up from among lower-growing planting – foxtail lilies (*Eremurus* spp.), with their heads packed with thousands of flowers, are some of the most effective of all. Foxgloves (*Digitalis* spp.) can do so, too, and the white foxglove (*D. purpurea* f. *albiflora*) growing against a backdrop of dark trees or shade is especially beautiful.

Other perennials can be used as seasonal key plants because of the way they combine stature with shape. Some of the larger members of the cow-parsley family, such as *Angelica archangelica*, do wonders for the self-esteem of borders, their upward-thrusting stems carrying heads of radiating flower stems. Others, such as plume poppy (*Macleaya* spp.), have that quality of presence we are looking for because they combine large size with elegantly shaped leaves and, in the greyish foliage of these particular plants, a distinctive colour.

The larger ornamental grasses are also very useful for creating seasonal architecture. *Miscanthus sinensis* grows to around 2m (over 6ft), and carries elegant plumes of seed through the winter, while species of *Molinia* are somewhat smaller with a more subtle 'starburst' of leaves and flower stems. While miscanthus consorts well with other large plants, molinias need space around them to look their best.

The Exotic Look

'Hardy exotics' have been quite a growth area recently, the selling-point being that here is a group of plants that look as if they belong in the rainforest but that can, in fact, be grown in anyone's garden. The hard fact is, however, that many of them are not reliably hardy in all areas, and most will be severely damaged by very cold or strong winds. Nevertheless, if they are carefully chosen, such plants can be highly effective in providing impact in gardens. One really striking, tropical-looking plant can make all the difference to a border, lifting it well and truly out of the mundane.

Some gardeners like to go one stage further and take their borders into the realms of fantasy, with more extensive pseudo-tropical-looking planting. It is all a question of taste. To some eyes the juxtaposition of lots of plants with large and dramatic leaves is too 'busy' and disordered, or leads to questions about where the monkeys are. To others, it is the most exciting thing that can be done in a garden. It is also possible to add exotic spice to a border by planting out conservatory and half-hardy plants over the summer.

The chapters on Containers and 'Instant' Gardens will provide you with lots more ideas for adding a touch of the exotic to your garden.

Playing with Shape

We have noted how black and white photographs are a good way to start analysing the structural components of your garden, enabling you better to appreciate the shape of plants and the different textures of foliage. Large-leaved plants will stand out from among surrounding small-leaved varieties. Line drawings of plant outlines are another way to appreciate shape and do not require much skill. This exercise will help you to understand how combinations of shape seem inherently more satisfying than others.

A planting that combines several different shapes is seen by most eyes as more interesting than one that consists of only one shape – a planting of heathers might be jolly and colourful, for example, but it will be transformed by the addition of just one upright conifer or a couple of wispy grasses. A border of tall, erect perennials looks less satis-fying than one where there is a mixture of upright and low, clumpy shapes. In addition, most upright perennials have

Outline drawings are one way of learning how to appreciate combinations of shapes.

Too many plants of the same shape can seem monotonous or unattractive.

A planting that brings together several different shapes is more harmonious.

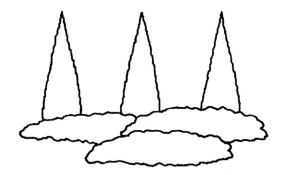

Juxtaposing radically different shapes, without anything intermediate, creates a sense of dynamism and energy.

Livening up Monotonous Planting

Problem

• Too many later flowering, tall, erect-growing varieties in a perennial border.

Solution

• The addition of clump-forming varieties, such as geraniums, dwarf asters, euphorbias and so on, or of low-growing shrubs, many of which have the advantage also of being evergreen. Species of lavender, cistus, santolina, cytisus and daphne could be used.

The addition of clump-forming perennials and shrubs in front of taller perennials complements them, hides lower bare stems and, if species tolerant of light shade are planted between them, helps to reduce weeding, too.

Problem

• All low-growing heathers or spreading conifers

Solution

• The addition of both more upright conifers, such as Irish juniper (*Juniperus communis* 'Hibernica'), *Thuja orientalis* 'Aurea Nana' or *Chamaecyparis obtusa* 'Nana Pyramidalis', and some grasses, which add a light ethereal touch. Cultivars of *Molinia caerulea* and *Deschampsia flexuosa* grow alongside heathers naturally.

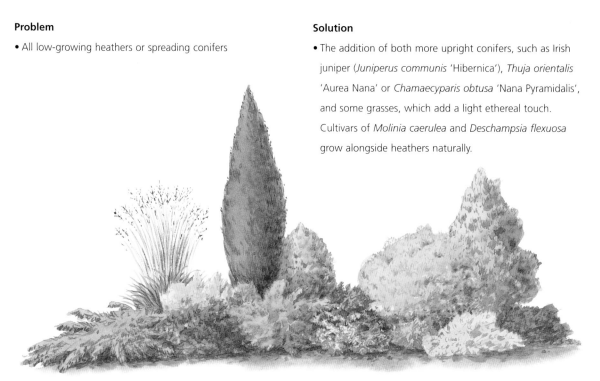

Contrasting shapes can make all the difference to arrangements of low-growing plants.

Problem

• Ground-cover perennials in shade all growing to around the same height.

Solution

• The use of some taller growing, shade-tolerant plants to add interest. *Carex pendula*, a sedge with elegantly pendant flowerheads, grows somewhat taller than most shade growers, and both it and male fern (*Dryopteris filix-mas*) are tolerant of dry shade. In reasonably moist shade, a wider variety of ferns with an upright vase-shaped profile can be used, such as the shuttlecock fern (*Matteuccia struthiopteris*).

Taller ferns and sedges can be added to grow among low ground cover in shade.

Problem

• A shrub border is composed of varieties that have a similar rounded habit.

Solution

• The addition of a few shrubs with an upright habit will 'vary the pace' somewhat; examples include species of *Holodiscus*, *Sorbaria* and *Rubus,* and also *Neillia thibetica* and *Leycesteria formosa*. If the soil is reasonably moist and the site is sheltered from strong winds, consider using bamboos, whose habit and foliage contrast perfectly with the shapes of woody shrubs.

Upright and arching habits make an ideal contrast to the shape of most shrubs.

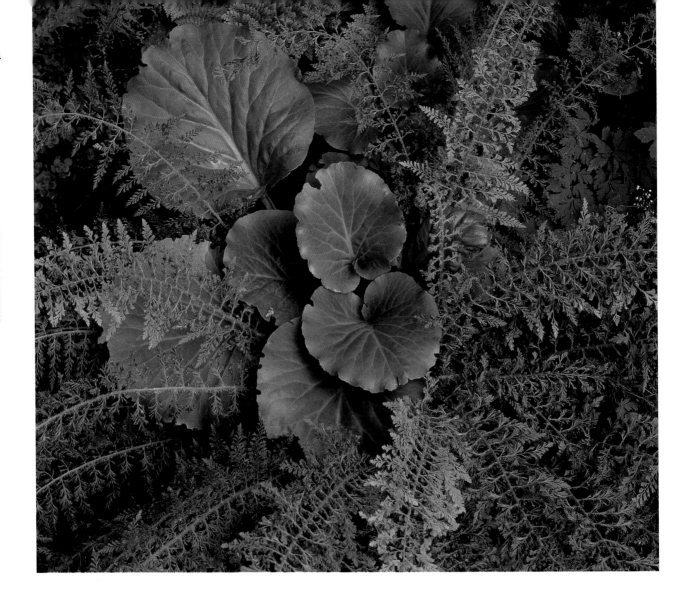

Two shade-tolerant plants, a bergenia and a fern, illustrate how glossy and matt textured leaves can create interesting contrasts.

rather unattractive 'bare legs' by the time they flower, and lower plants can cover them.

Most plants have a pretty amorphous shape, shrubs perhaps more than most. The addition of a few species that have distinct shapes or that offer some radically different quality can make all the difference. Adding too many different shapes, however, can have an over-stimulating result.

Texture

Texture can refer both to the overall appearance of a plant and to the look and feel of foliage close up. As an example of the first quality, think about how different are laurel (*Prunus laurocerasus*), with its big glossy leaves, and fennel (*Foeniculum vulgare*), whose foliage is a mass of finely divided leaves. The former reflects light, so appearing glossy; the latter absorbs it, so looking matt. Effective planting combines plants with both qualities. Too much gloss, and the results are distracting and demanding; too much matt and the garden is dull.

The texture of individual leaves is also important when we consider plants close up. An area where space is limited, such as a courtyard, or where we tend to look at plants close to, such as around a door or next to a seating area, benefits from having plants with interestingly textured leaves. Some, such as the crimson glory vine (*Vitis coignetiae*) or the luxuriantly growing, moisture-loving rodgersias, have leaves with an interesting texture resulting from the patterns made by the veins. Others, such as the well-known lamb's ear (*Stachys byzantina*) or the mulleins (*Verbascum* spp.), are densely furry.

Instant 'Focus of Attention' Plants

Some plants grab the onlooker's attention with bright flowers. The following do so by having a highly distinct habit of growth or outstanding foliage.

Fritillaria imperialis
(crown imperial)

• Bulb
• 120 x 30cm (4ft x 12in)
• This plant is quite unlike anything else – it can be difficult to believe that it is a real plant, with its upright stems topped with dusky orange or yellow flowers beneath a topknot of leaves. Immensely stately, it is the ultimate late spring or early summer eye-catcher.
• Good drainage and full sun are essential.

Melianthus major
(honey locust)

• Evergreen shrub, herbaceous perennial
• 3 x 1.5m (10ft x 5ft), ultimately
• This is simply the finest hardy foliage plant. The gorgeous, large silver pinnate leaves are dramatically toothed. But, only just hardy, the plant needs some insulating cover in many areas and should be sited against a warm wall. Don't be tempted to let it grow as a shrub because it rapidly develops bare stems and looks terribly tatty; cut it back annually.
• Plant in full sun and any reasonably well-drained soil.

Miscanthus sinensis

• Herbaceous grass
• 2.2 x 0.8m (7ft x 32in) ultimately
• These large ornamental grasses, like very, very refined versions of pampas grass, have silver or pink-tinged plumes from late summer or autumn until late winter. They perhaps look their best in low, cold sunshine. There are now many varieties becoming available, varying greatly in size, with some as short as 50cm (20in). Combine miscanthus with large perennials for a striking late-season effect.
• Plant in full sun and any reasonable soil. It likes moisture but tolerates some drought once it becomes established, and is wind resistant.

Trachycarpus fortunei

• Evergreen palm
• 10 x 2m (33 x 6ft) ultimately
• If you want a palm tree, this is the one to have. It is hardy to -14°C (6°F), and looks good and exotic, even when quite young. Its speed of growth into a proper palm depends greatly on climate. It can look out of place unless surrounded by other exotic-looking plants.
• Plant in full sun and any reasonably well-drained soil. Keep out of strong and cold winds.

Yucca

• Evergreen shrub
• 4 x 4m (13 x 13ft) ultimately
• Spiky rosettes add a touch of drama and the desert to the garden, and after a few years it has spectacular spikes of white flowers. *Y. filamentosa* and *Y. gloriosa* are the most frequently seen species.
• Plant in full sun and well-drained or dry soil. It is remarkably hardy for something that looks so exotic.

Further suggestions

Abies koreana (Korean fir); *Acanthus* spp.; *Aciphylla* spp.; *Agave* spp.; *Angelica archangelica*; *Aralia* spp.; *Cardiocrinum giganteum*; *Cortaderia selloana* (pampas grass); *Corylus avellana* 'Contorta'; *Cynara cardunculus*; *Osmunda regalis*; *Paulownia* spp.; *Phormium tenax*

Yucca filamentosa 'Variegata'

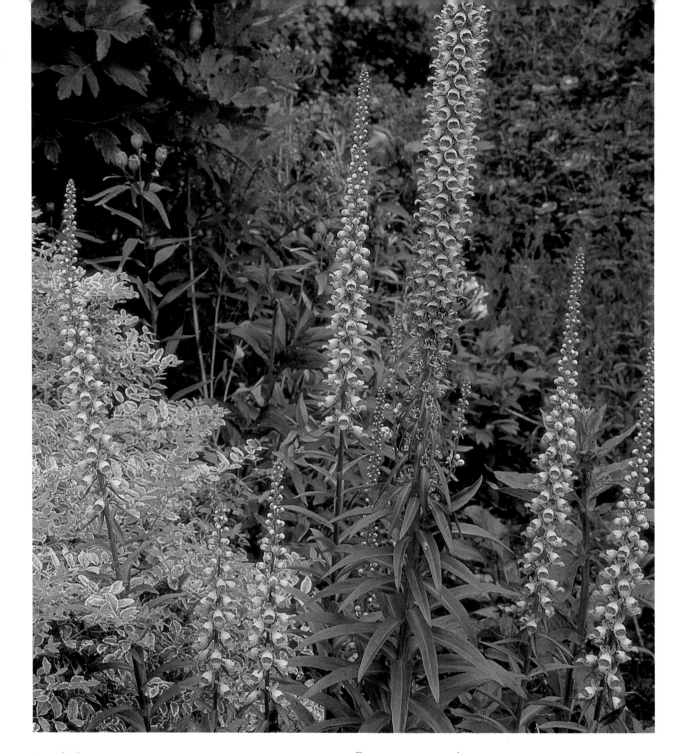

Digitalis ferruginea

Strong Verticals

Adding a strongly upright element is one of the simplest ways to transform ground-hugging borders or gardens. Upright plants need not be particularly tall, and small gardens often benefit from the use of those that aren't tall. Note that a tight, narrow shape emphasizes upright qualities dramatically.

Cupressus sempervirens
(Italian cypress)

• Evergreen coniferous tree

• 15 x 2.3m (50ft x 7ft 6in) ultimately

• Starring on every picture postcard from Tuscany, this narrow tree, with its dark foliage, is hardier than people think, as long as it is kept out of cold winds and protected with some sort of winter screening when it is young.

• Plant in any well-drained soil in full sun, including dry ones.

Digitalis ferruginea
(rusty foxglove)
- Short-lived herbaceous perennial
- 2 x 0.3m (6 x 1ft)
- Narrow spires of tightly packed, intricately marked, browny flowers make this a dramatic plant for sun or light shade. Like all foxgloves, it self-seeds, and colonies are soon built up.
- Grow in any reasonable soil.

Eremurus
(foxtail lily)
- Bulbous perennials
- 2 x 0.3m (6 x 1ft)
- With their tall spikes covered with thousands of tiny flowers, the foxtail lilies are among the most striking of bulbous plants.
- Good drainage and full sun essential. Enjoys hot, dry situations.

Juniperus scopulorum
'Skyrocket'
- Evergreen coniferous tree
- 8 x 0.8m (26ft x 32in)
- Very much like a grey-leaved version of the Italian cypress, this is more suitable for cold continental climates and for situations where a smaller eventual size is required. *J. communis* 'Hibernica' is smaller, 3 x 0.3m (10 x 1ft), and slow growing.

Verbascum bombyciferum
- Biennial
- 2 x 0.4m (6ft x 16in)
- Nearly all the verbascums (known as mulleins) are good vertical plants, their dead stems surviving resolutely upright through the winter. This species has densely woolly grey foliage and, like nearly all others, yellow flowers densely packed on a tall spike.
- Grow in full sun and any soil. It will happily self-seed.

Further suggestions
Allium giganteum and similar *Allium* spp. (onion); *Asphodeline lutea* (syn. *Asphodelus luteus*); *Calamagrostis* x *acutiflora* 'Karl Foerster' (syn. *C. stricta*); *Chamaecyparis lawsoniana* 'Kilmacurragh'; *Delphinium* hybrids; *Kniphofia* spp.; *Ligularia* 'The Rocket'; *Veronicastrum virginicum*

Interesting Foliage Texture
Very glossy or matt or otherwise textured leaves are a good way of contributing interest to plantings, and they provide another dimension close to.

Bergenia
(elephant's ear)
- Spreading, clump-forming evergreen perennials
- 30 x 50cm (12 x 20cm)
- Round, glossy evergreen leaves and very early flowers make bergenias invaluable plants for bringing life to the border in winter. They can also be used as ground cover. Some, especially *B. purpurascens*, turn a bronze-red colour in winter. Flowers vary from a rather demanding deep pink – *B.* 'Sunningdale', for example – to pure white – as in *B.* 'Silberlicht'.
- Grow in sun or light shade and any reasonable soil. Some dry shade is tolerated.

Foeniculum vulgare
(fennel)
- Erect-growing herbaceous perennial
- 2 x 0.5m (6ft x 20in)
- Very fine, dark green foliage gives fennel a very matt appearance, which is a distinct contrast to surrounding foliage. Small, yellow sheep's parsley-type flowers are borne in summer. The dark bronze form (*F. v.* 'Purpureum') accentuates further the light-absorbing quality of the plant.
- Grow in full sun and any reasonable soil.

Magnolia grandiflora
(southern magnolia)
- Evergreen tree
- 15 x 10m (50 x 33ft) ultimately in warm summer climates only
- Large, glossy leaves in a distinct shade of yellow-green have made this magnolia popular as a wall shrub for over 200 years, but it is perfectly hardy as a free-standing, slow-growing tree or as a clipped specimen. Huge white flowers are borne in late summer on mature plants.
- Grow in full sun in any reasonable soil. Wind protection is vital.

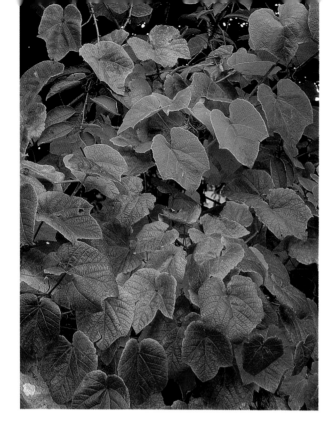

Vitis coignetiae

Vitis coignetiae
(crimson glory vine)

- Deciduous climber
- 12 x 12m (40 x 40ft) ultimately
- A favourite of Japanese classical painters, this magnificent vine needs plenty of space (like a large tree or an extensive wall) in order to develop its true potential. The large, roughly textured leaves turn red in autumn.
- Grow in full sun and any reasonable soil.

Further suggestions

Acacia dealbata (mimosa, silver wattle); *Acer palmatum* var. *dissectum*; *Alchemilla mollis* (lady's mantle); *Bassia scoparia* (syn. *Kochia scoparia*; summer cypress) *Carpinus betulus* (common hornbeam); *Ceanothus thyrsiflorus*; *Chamaecyparis obtusa* (Hinoki cypress); *Chamaerops humilis*; *Colletia* spp.; *Cytisus* (broom); *Eriobotrya japonica* (loquat, Japanese medlar); *Griselinia littoralis* (broadleaf); *Hebe* spp. (shrubby veronica); *Liriope* spp.; *Myrrhis odorata* (sweet cicely); *Phlomis* spp.; *Salvia officinalis* (sage); *Tamarix* spp. (tamarisk); *Veratrum* spp. (false hellebore); all ferns

Easy-to-clip Shrubs
The following are the traditional favourites for clipping into shapes, small or large, although the majority are slow growing. Some less frequently used, but promising, species are also included.

Buxus sempervirens
(box)

- Evergreen shrub
- 4 x 4m (13 x 13ft) ultimately if unclipped
- Box, with its small, densely packed, rounded leaves is the most popular subject for clipping into shapes. The variety *B. s.* 'Suffruticosa' is slower growing and thus more suitable for very low hedging.
- Grow in full sun or light shade and in fertile soil.

Euonymus japonicus

- Evergreen shrub
- 4 x 4m (13 x 13ft) ultimately if unclipped
- Glossy, rounded leaves are borne on compact shrubs that flourish in mild and maritime localities. Cold winds and hard frosts rule it out for many areas, however.
- Plant in sun, in any reasonable and sandy soil.

Laurus nobilis
(bay laurel, bay)

- Evergreen shrub
- 5 x 4m (16 x 13ft) ultimately if unclipped
- This is the culinary bay, a favourite plant for growing as a standard or clipping into spirals and other shapes. It has larger leaves than the others listed.
- Grow in sun, sheltered from cold wind and hard frost, in any reasonable soil.

Lonicera nitida
(box-leaved honeysuckle)

- Evergreen shrub
- 2 x 4m (6 x 13ft) ultimately if unclipped
- A rather down-market image has prevented this shrub, with its tiny dark leaves, being used more widely. It can be clipped to shape extremely well, the only drawback being that in larger specimens it may lose leaves lower down.
- Grow in sun or light shade and in any reasonable soil.

Taxus baccata

(yew)

• Evergreen coniferous tree

• 15 x 10m (50 x 33ft) ultimately if unclipped

• The dark foliage of yew is the classic backdrop for herbaceous borders and formal gardens. The trees bear red berries in autumn. *T. b.* 'Fastigiata' is the upright-growing variety.

• Plant in full sun or light shade and in any reasonable soil. Yew will flourish on thin alkaline soils but grows better on fertile ones.

Further suggestions

Baccharis patagonica; *Ceanothus thyrsiflorus*; *Elaeagnus* x *ebbingei*; *Hebe parvifolia* var. *angustifolia*; *Ligustrum delavayanum*; *Viburnum tinus* (laurustinus)

Big, Exotic Foliage

Creating the bold, tropical look in your garden is easy enough to do with the following hardy, or almost hardy, exotics.

Arundo donax

• Slowly spreading herbaceous grass

• 3m (10ft)

• This is the huge reed that takes over ditches in many Mediterranean countries. In cooler climates it makes a magnificent, if somewhat untidy, plant for hardy exotic plantings.

• Plant in full sun, away from cold and windy sites, in fertile and preferably damp soil.

Clematis armandii

• Evergreen climber

• 8 x 8m (26 x 26ft)

• Exotic-looking evergreen foliage make this clematis one of the most valuable of all climbers, especially when it flowers in spring with large bunches of white flowers.

• A vigorous grower in full sun and any reasonable soil. It is hardy but dislikes cold winds.

Fatsia japonica

• Evergreen shrub

• 4 x 4m (13 x 13ft)

• Large, 40cm (16in), hand-shaped leaves and a compact habit produce a plant ideal for exotic courtyard planting, especially since it does well in light shade. Cream flowers, rather like giant ivy blossom, appear in late summer.

• Plant in any reasonable soil.

Gunnera

• Slowly spreading, clump-forming herbaceous perennials

• 1.8 x 2.5m (5ft 6in x 8ft)

• This is the vast giant rhubarb that always seems to lurk by expanses of water in the gardens of stately homes. *G. manicata* (giant rhubarb) is the species normally seen; *G. tinctoria* (syn. *G. scabra*) is two-thirds the size.

• Plant in sun or light shade, in moist, reasonably fertile soil. It is hardy, although in cold climates the dead leaves can be heaped over the buds for winter protection.

Musa basjoo

• Evergreen perennial

• 2 x 1m (6 x 3ft)

• The almost hardy banana makes its surroundings instantly tropical, with paddle-shaped leaves almost a metre (yard) long. The root is hardy, the top not, so wrapping the stems in bubble plastic or other insulating material is essential if the plant it to build up height over the years.

• Plant in full sun, in well-drained but moist soil. Fertile soil is essential for good results.

Further suggestions

Acanthus spp. (bear's breeches); *Ailanthus altissima*; *Aralia* spp.; *Aristolochia macrophylla* (syn. *A. durior*); *Blechnum tabulare*; *Ficus carica* (common fig); *Hosta* large-leaved varieties; *Hydrangea aspera* Villosa Group (syn. *H. villosa*), *H. macrophylla*; *Kalopanax* spp.; *Lobelia tupa*; *Lysichiton* spp.; *Miscanthus floridulus*, *M. sacchariflorus*; *Paulownia* spp.; *Petasites japonicus* var. *japonicus*; *Rheum* spp.; *Ricinus communis*; *Tetrapanax papyrifer*; *Yucca* spp.; all bamboos

Specimen plants

Specimen plants stand either on their own, or in a superior and more central position to those around them. They should be plants that you especially like or feel proud of, and should look good on their own and for as much of the year as possible. A good specimen plant is nearly always one with some architectural interest, and if it has good flowers or fruit or some other features, all the better. There is not much point having a beautiful flowering shrub as a specimen or centrepiece to a planting if it is going to look like an amorphous blob for most of the year.

There is no doubt about the key role that specimen plants play in transforming the whole area around them, or indeed the whole garden or perhaps even the neighbourhood. The larger the space, the larger should be the specimen plant, and in small gardens a clipped shrub or fine architectural perennial might be used.

Specimen Trees

While the altruistic might want to plant a cedar (*Cedrus* spp.) or Californian redwood (*Sequoiadendron giganteum*) for future generations, most of us want something that will grow a little more quickly to create a specimen for a large space. There are a few really fine trees that are sufficiently fast growing to give results in ten years, notably the Hungarian oak (*Quercus frainetto*) and especially any of the wing-nut trees (*Pterocarya* spp.), which grow incredibly quickly to reach a majestic size within 25 years. The Monterey pine (*Pinus radiata*; syn. *P. insignis*), commonly

Above: *Magnolia* x *soulangeana* is one of the most dramatic of all spring-flowering small trees, making it ideal for places where it stands in splendid isolation.

planted as a coastal windbreak, is perhaps the best fast and magnificent conifer, followed by the monkey puzzle (*Araucaria araucana*).

Of small and medium-sized trees there are a good many readily available: maples (*Acer* spp.) are popular for their brilliant autumn colour and the attractive bark of some; birches (*Betula* spp.) are grown for their graceful habit and bark; cherries (*Prunus* spp.) offer flowers and bark, and apples (*Malus* spp.) have flowers, fruit and sometimes autumn colour. All these are attractive trees, but only a few have a really fine form, which may be essential if their context is to be a formal one. In some cases, notably the somewhat upright and loose-growing birches, it may be better, if space allows, to plant several close together to make a small stand than to grow one on its own.

Perhaps the small tree with the most exceptional shape is the table dogwood (*Cornus controversa*), with its 'wedding cake', layered branching pattern. It is one of those plants that just has to be grown as a specimen if it not to be insulted. The upright form of the common hornbeam (*Carpinus betulus* 'Fastigiata'), which sends up a veritable forest of upright, thrusting branches, is another.

Specimen Shrubs

Shrubs with such fine form that they make obvious specimen plants are few and far between. In settings where formality is important, it is not really appropriate to grow them on their own, although an exception might be made for those that can be relied on to form a symmetrical shape. It is not surprising that formal gardens usually use clipped trees and shrubs, such as yew, instead of naturally shaped plants.

There are, however, many shrubs that are commonly grown as specimens surrounded by mown grass in informal garden settings. I always think this produces something of the piecemeal effect of a botanical garden, but it is undeniably a lower maintenance approach than mixing in perennials. Part of the unsatisfactory aspect of this kind of planting is simply that the majority of shrubs have indistinct shapes – they are, by nature, plants that grow together and the 'shrub border' is a much more natural way to grow them. There are some that are worth growing on their own, however. Many of the viburnums not only develop a good shape but have multiple reasons to be grown and admired in splendid isolation – flowers, foliage, fruit and autumn colour.

Perennials as Specimen Plants

Large perennials can be used as specimen plants in lawns, and this is, in fact, a good way of preventing some of the more invasive ones from spreading, as their suckers are cut down by mowing – the truly magnificent *Macleaya microcarpa*, for example, can become a menace in a border. Large and majestic perennials can also be grown as the key plants in borders, although they are shown off best if the plants surrounding them are less than half their height. It is a good general rule that if you are growing any plant whose overall form you are trying to emphasize, it will be appreciated better if it grown among much lower growing plants.

It was common in Victorian times to grow large half-hardy foliage plants as the centrepieces in bedding plant schemes. The same practice is being revived today with

Shapes for specimen shrubs

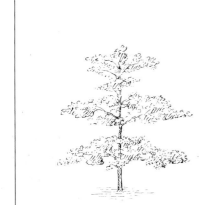

Layered

such as *Cornus controversa*

and *Viburnum plicatum*

Upright and arching

such as *Chusquea culeou*

and *Leycesteria formosa*

Rounded

such as *Euphorbia mellifera*

the use of such plants as palms, cannas and bananas. It is possible, however, to take this idea and adapt it to hardy plants using large-leaved species, such as the fatsia or species of aralia. The use of spiky-leaved species like cordylines has already been noted (see page 48).

Selecting Specimen Plants

Knowing the ultimate size of a potential specimen plant and how quickly it is going to achieve those dimensions is important; it is equally important to be completely sure that the plant is suitable for the conditions in which it is to be grown. A yellowing or wind-battered plant that is half hidden in a border is one thing; a similar plant grown in the best position in the garden is quite another.

Trees with fine trunks or beautiful bark benefit from being grown on their own or, at least, surrounded by nothing higher than ground cover. Others might benefit from having other plants around them – perennials, for example, will perhaps lengthen the season of interest. If the centrepiece is deciduous, the inclusion of evergreens or some winter-flowering species would be beneficial.

Formal, very architectural settings benefit from symmetrical specimen plants with a clearly defined shape. This kind of plant is often more appropriate for a small garden or space, as are those with a narrow profile or upright-growing branches. More amorphous and bulkier shapes tend to look better in larger, informal settings, such as in extensive lawns or where there are views over the countryside.

Left: A well grown hosta, especially a variegated one, makes a good specimen plant in smaller places. Its rosette of broad leaves provide a good contrast with a mass of more indistinct leaves.

Above: Some trees, such as this *Prunus serrula*, have the most exquisitely beautiful bark. They need careful positioning so that they can be properly admired.

Plant Directory

Evergreens

The following plants include some of the most striking of all garden evergreens, which need to be seen in situations where they can be appreciated without the distraction of surrounding planting.

Araucaria araucana

(monkey puzzle, Chile pine)

- Evergreen coniferous tree
- 20 x 15m (66 x 50ft) ultimately
- If, repeat if, you have the space for it, the monkey puzzle is one of the finest of hardy trees, looking both extraordinary and magnificent right from the word go. The stems are clad in large, thick, green scales.
- Grow in sun and any reasonable soil. It is a good choice for westerly maritime climates.

Arbutus

(strawberry tree)

- Evergreen small tree
- 15 x 15m (50 x 50ft) ultimately
- An elegantly branching habit makes the strawberry trees good and unusual evergreens. They have small white flowers and reddish, strawberry-like fruits in autumn. As they age, the trees develop peeling, cinnamon-toned bark. *A. x andrachnoides* and *A. unedo* are the common ones; *A. marina* is the fastest growing.
- Does best in mild climates and is certainly not for cold, windy ones. Grow in sun and any reasonable soil, including thin, alkaline ones.

Picea breweriana

Eucryphia

- Evergreen small tree
- Generally upright growing, with dark grey-green leaves, the eucryphias can astonish when they flower in midsummer and the plant is smothered in quite large white flowers. *E. x nymansensis*, 8 x 4m (26 x 13ft), is popular and reliable.
- It does best in mild areas, preferably in acid soil.

Picea breweriana

(Brewer's weeping spruce)

- Evergreen coniferous tree
- 10 x 6m (33 x 20ft)
- Pendant branches with blue-green needles make this stand out as one of the most beautiful of the spruces.
- Somewhat slow to get going; plant in sun and any reasonable soil.

Picea omorika

(Serbian spruce)

- Evergreen coniferous tree
- 16 x 3m (53 x 10ft)
- This, the narrowest spruce of all, is an exceptionally elegant tree and is spectacular if several are grown as a small group.
- Plant in sun and any reasonable soil. This is the only spruce for thin, alkaline soils.

Shapely Shrubs

Few shrubs can be recommended for their shape alone; the following have a better claim than most.

Chusquea culeou

(Chilean bamboo)

- Evergreen bamboo
- 5 x 3m (16 x 10ft)
- One of the most elegant of a graceful group, chusquea's arching stems are best appreciated when it is grown as a specimen clump rather than being hemmed in by anything else.
- Plant in sun or light shade and in soil that is well drained but moist. Chusquea dislikes wind.

Euphorbia mellifera
(syn. *E. longifolia*)

- Evergreen shrub/small tree

- 3 x 3m (10 x 10ft) ultimately, in mild areas only

- A beautifully rounded shrub, with honey-scented flowers in early spring and light green leaves. It can also be trained as a standard.

- Not reliably hardy in cold areas, it needs a sheltered site but will grow anywhere.

Hydrangea aspera subsp. *sargentiana*

- Deciduous suckering shrub

- 2.5 x 2m (8 x 6ft)

- No one seeing this shrub in winter would describe it as shapely: it is just a bunch of upright sticks. In spring, however, huge, hairy leaves are produced and in early summer delicate lavender-coloured, lacecap flowerheads, making it exotic and grand.

- Plant in sun or light shade, and in any reasonable soil that is preferably not dry.

Viburnum plicatum

- Deciduous shrub

- 5 x 5m (16 x 16ft)

- Layered branches make this shrub stand out whatever the time of year, but it is at its best in late spring with its lacecap, cream flowerheads. *V. p.* 'Mariesii' has the best tiered habit and is smaller.

- It does best in light shade in any reasonable soil.

Further suggestions

Acer palmatum small varieties; *Aralia elata* (Japanese angelica tree); *Clerodendron trichotomum*; *Embothrium coccineum* (Chilean fire bush); *Fatsia japonica*; *Fremontondendron californicum*; *Genista aetnensis* (Mount Etna broom); *Griselinia littoralis* (broadleaf); *Ilex* spp. (holly); *Mahonia* spp.; *Myrtus communis* (common myrtle); *Pittosporum tenuifolium*; *Rhododendron yakushimanum*; *Yucca* spp.

Small Trees that Stay Small
Many is the garden that would look better with a tree, but the choice is so often limited by what can be fitted in. The following are particularly distinguished and stay small.

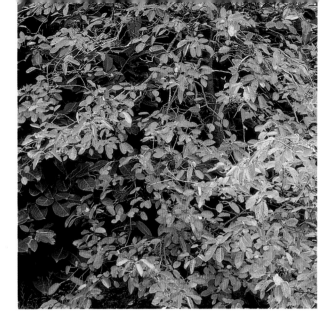

Amelanchier canadensis

Amelanchier canadensis

- Deciduous small tree

- 8 x 6m (26 x 20ft)

- This versatile tree has white flowers in spring, followed by purple berries and orange foliage in autumn.

- Plant in sun or very light shade and in any reasonable soil. It thrives in damp conditions.

Betula
(birch)

- Deciduous small trees

- 12 x 5m (40 x 16ft)

- Renowned for their bark, birches have relatively light growth and do not cast heavy shade. *B. utilis* var. *jacquemontii* (West Himalayan birch) has excellent white bark and a good habit, *B. albosinensis* (white Chinese birch) has particularly beautiful pink bark.

- Plant in sun and in any reasonable soil; birches will even grow in infertile soils. They are very cold hardy.

Cornus controversa
(table dogwood)

- Deciduous small tree

- 7 x 6m (23 x 20ft)

- The 'wedding cake' branching pattern of this tree, with gaps between the layers, is highly distinctive, making it a definite talking-point. *C. c.* 'Variegata' has cream-variegated foliage.

- Plant in sun or light shade, in any reasonable soil, although it will do best in deep, rich soil.

Halesia
(snowdrop tree, silverbell tree)
- Deciduous small tree
- 6 x 6m (20 x 20ft)
- In spring the snowdrop trees have attractive little white pendant flowers, which are delicate and unusual. *H. monticola* (mountain snowdrop tree) is the most tree-like, while the other species are more shrubby.
- Grow in moist but well-drained, acid soil in sun or very light shade.

Malus tschonoskii
- Deciduous small tree
- 12 x 4m (40 x 13ft)
- A neat vase-shaped habit has made this a favourite tree for many urban streets, and it seems tailormade for small gardens. It bears white blossom in spring and has good orange autumn colour.
- Plant in full sun and in any reasonable soil.

Stewartia
- Deciduous small tree
- 10 x 5m (33 x 16ft)
- Related to camellias, of which their spring-borne white flowers are reminiscent, stewartias are characterized by attractive foliage and cinnamon bark. They have very striking autumn colour. *S. pseudocamellia* is the most often grown.
- Plant in sun or very light shade. Acid soil is essential; it should be moist but well drained. Not suitable for cold climates.

Eupatorium purpureum 'Atropurpureum'

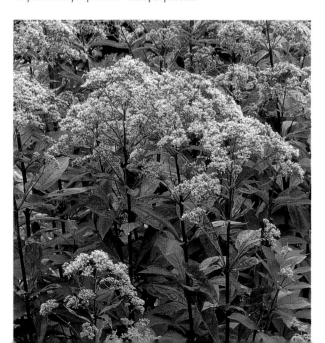

Further suggestions

Acer griseum (paper-bark maple); *Buddleja alternifolia*; *Cercis siliquastrum* (Judas tree); *Crataegus* spp. (hawthorn); *Ilex* spp. (holly): *Laburnum* spp.; *Ligustrum lucidum* (Chinese privet); *Magnolia* spp.; *Malus* spp.; *Paulownia* spp.; *Prunus* spp.; *Rhus* spp. (sumac); *Sorbus* spp.

Specimen Perennials
The following make fine centrepieces for island beds or other perennial plantings, or just for growing surrounded by grass.

Angelica archangelica
(angelica)
- Erect-growing biennial
- 2 x 1m (6 x 3ft)
- A vast and very superior cow parsley-type plant, with yellow-green flowerheads. Usually biennial, it can be kept going by removing the dead flowers and thus preventing seeding. It is, however, easy to propagate from seed.
- Grow in sun or light shade and in any reasonable soil.

Eupatorium purpureum
'Atropurpureum' (Joe Pye weed)
- Slowly spreading, clump-forming herbaceous perennial
- 2 x 1m (6 x 3ft)
- Tall, purple-stained stems carry fluffy pink flowerheads in mid- to late summer, attracting many butterflies. Although very upright, further stems are produced as the clump builds up over the years.
- Plant in sun and in any reasonable soil; it does best on moist soil.

Macleaya cordata
(syn. *Bocconia cordata*; plume poppy, tree celandine)
- Spreading, clump-forming perennial
- 2 x 1m (6 x 3ft)
- Grey leaves, vaguely reminiscent of the fig, and a magnificent habit combine in midsummer with plumes of tiny flowers atop the stems. *M. microcarpa* (syn. *Bocconia microcarpa*) is almost identical but suckers strongly, so grow it surrounded by mown grass.
- Plant in sun and in any reasonable soil.

Rheum palmatum
'Atrosanguineum'
• Clump-forming perennial
• 2 x 1m (6 x 3ft), 1m (3ft) tall after flowering
• A majestic rhubarb, with bronze-red-stained, jagged-edged foliage and a tall spike of creamy flowers in spring.
• Grow in sun and in any reasonable soil, although moisture and fertility will bring much the best results.

Stipa gigantea
(golden oats)
• Clump-forming evergreen grass
• 2 x 1m (6 x 3ft)
• Panicles of oat-like flower- and seedheads appear from early summer on. Its 'transparent' nature makes this a good mixer with other lower growing perennials. It does need space around it if it is to be seen at its best.
• Plant in sun and in any reasonable soil. It is good on dry, poor soils.

Further suggestions

Aruncus dioicus (syn. *A. plumosus, A. sylvestris, A. vulgaris*); *Crocosmia paniculata* (syn. *Antholyza coccinea, A. paniculata, Curtonus paniculatus*); *Echinops* spp. (globe thistle); *Ferula communis* (giant fennel); *Filipendula rubra*; *Inula* spp.; *Miscanthus* spp.; *Paeonia* larger varieties; *Rheum* spp.; *Rodgersia* spp.

Half-hardy Plants as Spectacular Specimens
If you want to follow Victorian practice and grow half-hardy exotics in bedding schemes for the summer months, the following are some of the most rewarding and readily available. Protection in winter will be necessary for most of them. Conservatory or even the not-too-tropical houseplants may be put outside for the summer.

Agave
• Evergreen perennials
• 2 x 2m (6 x 6ft) ultimately, in warm climates
• Aggressively spiny, agaves are favourite focal-point plants. They are best used in containers when small, but can be planted in the ground when larger, although great care needs to be exercised when handling them. The yellow-striped *A. americana* 'Mediopicta' is the most popular.
• Grow in full sun. Agaves have some drought tolerance but are not generally hardy.

Canna
• Herbaceous perennials
• 100 x 60cm (36 x 24in) average
• Popular for their exotic red, orange, yellow or pink flowers and for their broad leaves, arranged around a strongly upright stem, cannas are most effectively grown in a clump in summer plantings. *C. iridiflora*, which has deep pink flowers, is somewhat more elegant than the exuberant hybrids that are usually seen.
• Grow in sun and in fertile soil. Cannas are easily dug up and stored dry as tubers over the winter.

Cordyline australis
(New Zealand cabbage palm)
• Evergreen shrub
• 15 x 5m (50 x 16ft) ultimately, in warm climates
• The rosette of strap-shaped leaves makes cordylines perfect centrepiece plants. The dark-leaved variety *C. a.* 'Atropurpurea' is often seen planted in an urn.
• Grow in full sun and in any reasonable soil. Reliably hardy in milder sheltered areas only, cordylines are hardier if they are planted out in the ground.

Phoenix canariensis
(Canary Island date palm)
• Evergreen palm
• 2 x 2m (6 x 6ft) usual with container-grown plants
• A relative of the date palm, this is a good centrepiece plant where there is plenty of space for its wide, spreading, dark green, pinnate leaves to expand.
• Grow in sun and in any reasonable soil. This palm is not generally hardy outside.

Further suggestions

Cycas half-hardy spp.; *Dracaena* half-hardy spp.; *Ensete ventricosum*; *Schefflera* half-hardy spp.

Impact all year round

A garden that looks good all year round is the wish of many gardeners, and it is not an unreasonable desire, provided that sumptuous colour and complete perfection are not demanded of every single month. A garden that fulfils this criterion does require considerable organization to achieve, however, and the key, especially in small gardens, is the efficient use of space.

Spring is, perhaps, the easiest time to provide lots of cheerful colour, as bulbs are inexpensive, easy to grow and almost instantaneous in their effect. Early summer is also an easy season to fill with colour. Many gardeners, however, complain that late summer and autumn are 'difficult' times in the garden. The answer may lie more in fashion and in the availability of good late-season plants than in anything else.

Later season perennials are currently slowly creeping back after a period when they were distinctly out of favour, and many gardeners were unaware of their virtues. Annuals and bedding plants, the other main sources of later colour, are also undergoing a revolution, with the garish varieties disliked by many being joined by new introductions that are more subtle and natural looking.

Winter is not a time that gardeners should give up on. Not only is there the occasional flower, but there are shrubs with coloured bark, perennials with statuesque seedheads and evergreens in colours other than dark green.

Above: Traditional displays of spring colour such as this are dependent on a lot of planting the previous autumn – of tulip bulbs and wallflower and forget-me-not plants – but they are reliably showy.

Relying on Long-season Interest

Among the most useful garden plants are those that look good for long periods. They are especially valuable in the smaller garden, where plants that look brilliant for two weeks and a tatty mess for the next three months are not what is needed.

Unfortunately, flowers are, of course, inherently short lived, the majority of plants having a distinct and limited flowering season. It is true that the horticultural industry has done its best to breed varieties that flower all summer long, but all too often they combine this habit with harsh colouring and over-large flowers. A naturally long flowering season should be regarded as a bonus; it should not be expected.

The fact is that relatively few garden plants have flowering seasons that last for more than a month. Varieties with double flowers often flower for longer than the naturally occurring single ones, because double flowers often lack certain of the organs necessary for successful fertilization and, therefore, seed production. The plant carries on flowering in the vain hope that eventually seed might be produced. Double roses are a good example of this. Some single-flowering hybrids are also similarly sterile, in the way that a mule is – the perennial wallflower (*Erysimum* 'Bowles Mauve') is probably one such.

Autumn can be a very colourful time: the last of the summer flowers (*Rudbeckia* 'Goldsturm') bloom here alongside berries (*Euonymus planipes*) and turning leaves (*Cornus alba* 'Sibirica').

Most natural species that flower for a long period are annuals or perennials that are notably short lived, which is one reason for the popularity of these plants, although this characteristic has been greatly enhanced by intensive breeding over many years. Most annuals and short-lived perennials are native to dry or disturbed, stressful habitats. They flower quickly to produce enough seed to start another generation, just in case there is a drought around the corner that will wipe them out. If conditions continue to be good, they just carry on flowering.

It seems obvious, then, that annuals must not be stressed, otherwise they might finish flowering, make their final seeding and die. Grow them lushly, with plenty of water and they will carry on flowering. The same is true of short-lived perennials, such as South American vervain (*Verbena bonariensis*; syn. *V. patagonica*), which flowers for months in most garden.

What Else Does it do Apart from Flower?

It is easy to get carried away with impulse buying at garden centres and nurseries. It pays to consider carefully what that plant with lovely flowers that look so appealing next to the sales desk is going to look like in a few weeks' time. Try to imagine it without flowers. Is it worth having for the foliage alone? Is the foliage going to complement anything else in the garden? Or, is it just going to look nondescript – plain awful even?

A salutary exercise for the impulse-buy addict is to think about what a lot of popular garden plants look like when they are not in flower. Forsythia is an example – stunning in late winter and a source of great happiness to many, but what about the rest of the year? It is one of the most unshapely of shrubs and has poor quality foliage but a habit of growing so vigorously that plants nearby can be swamped. Mock orange (*Philadelphus* spp.) is similarly dull when it is not seducing us with its fragrant white flowers. If you do want to include these large-growing shrubs

Left: Some gardeners like to organize the garden so that different parts perform best at certain times. Archways covered in climbing roses associated with delphiniums provide a classic summer spectacle that takes up little space.

with such dull foliage and habit, think about how they can be more easily controlled as garden plants, growing them trained to a wall for instance (see the chapter on Assessing Your Garden, page 25).

While we are on the subject of popular plats that look thoroughly boring when they are not actually flowering, consider roses. Would anyone grow a rose for its foliage alone? A well-know Dutch garden designer, asked why he did not use roses in his work, replied: 'They have unattractive foliage and an awful shape.' In their defence, it has to be said that some roses do have good foliage, but it is only really worth having as a foil to the flowers.

Plants with a long season of interest can be divided into two categories: the first are those that are valuable for their architectural qualities or for the shape and colour of the foliage; the second are plants that are valuable because they perform more than once a year. We have already looked at architectural plants and varieties grown primarily for their foliage interest. Such plants are vital for bringing a sense of continuity to the garden.

But one can have too much continuity. This is the problem with all those low-maintenance evergreen conifer and heather gardens. Not enough happens, and you only know what time of year it is by which heathers happen to be in flower. For many people, who depend on gardens to give them a sense of experiencing nature, this is not enough – where is the march of the seasons, where is the dynamism of growth and change? These are the advantages of flowers, fruit and autumn colour. Plants that have all three, or in some other way look thoroughly desirable more than once a year, are popular partly for their marking of the passage of seasons.

Multi-season Plants

A plant may be multi-seasonal and multi-purpose in the garden if it provides interest at more than one season. Such plants are especially useful for small gardens, earning their keep twice over, so to speak.

FLOWERING AND FRUITING TREES AND SHRUBS
Any woody plant – and it is nearly always woody species – that produces attractive fruit is going to have to flower first, which makes it automatically a two-season plant. A

mountain ash (*Sorbus* spp.) or firethorn (*Pyracantha* spp.), with its white or cream flowers, is perhaps best described as 'quietly beautiful'; the flowers are certainly nothing compared to the stunning display of brightly coloured fruit that follows in autumn.

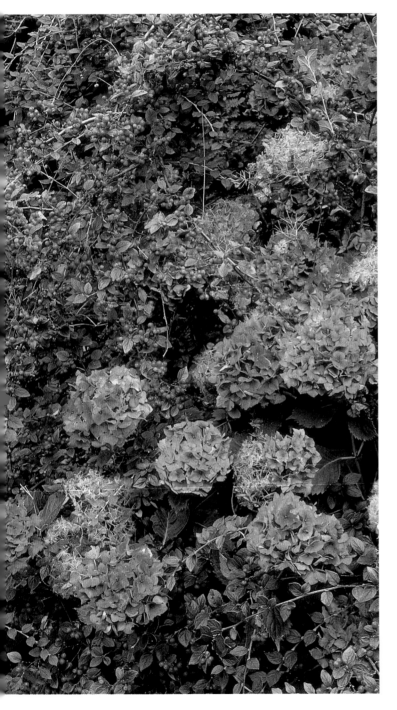

'Out of season' flowers can be surprising – here faded hydrangea flowers harmonize with cotoneaster berries.

Those trees and shrubs with genuinely more beautiful flowers as well as good fruit are definitely worth the multi-season tag; viburnums, hawthorns (*Crataegus* spp.) and ornamental crab apples (*Malus* spp.) are three such. The last is a reminder that the ultimate dual-purpose plants for the garden are fruit trees: apples, pears, cherries and plums. Personally, I rate the blended white and pink of apple blossom more highly than any ornamental cherry (*Prunus* spp.), and you can eat the proceeds a few months later. I sometimes wonder why ornamental cherries are so popular when most of them do not produce any ornamental – or edible – fruit. However, they do, at least, have good autumn colour.

FLOWERING AND FOLIAGE PERENNIALS

Many plants grown primarily for their flowers also have attractive foliage, as we have already noted. Some are especially useful, however. Varieties of deadnettle (*Lamium* spp.) and bugle (*Ajuga* spp.) flower in early spring and have attractive evergreen leaves as well, and both are first-rate ground-cover plants for lightly shaded places. Many shade-tolerant plants have good foliage – lungwort (*Pulmonaria* spp.) with its silver-splashed leaves, for example, and hellebores (*Helleborus* spp.) with their rather majestic clumps of hand-shaped leaves, which add structure to borders throughout the year.

FLOWERING SHRUBS WITH GOOD FOLIAGE

Most shrubs have leaves that are really rather nondescript, and this, combined with their overall lack of shape, is the explanation for what is, I confess, a certain lack of enthusiasm for shrubs on my part. There are, however, those that do have foliage of remarkable quality, which makes them genuinely two-season plants.

The dark, glossy, evergreen leaves, good habit and flowers make camellias attractive shrubs at all times; the Japanese even use them as hedging plants for this very reason, and pruning them reduces flowering drastically. Hydrangeas usually have good-sized, attractive leaves, and some have outstanding foliage. *Hydrangea quercifolia*, its leaves shaped approximately like those of an oak tree, is one example; *H. aspera* and *H. a.* Villosa Group have large hairy leaves that make them very distinctive and exotic looking.

It is, however, perhaps the rhododendrons that have some of the most attractive leaves of all flowering shrubs. Indeed, once upon a time a well-known rhododendron nursery staged an exhibit of them at a London flower show in August, with not a flower in sight, the stand consisting of a pyramid of species chosen for their leaves. It won a gold medal, and a certain amount of grumbling disapproval from fellow exhibitors. Many species have dense cinnamon-coloured 'fur' (properly called indumentum) on the young growth or the underside of the leaves. With others it is the size of the leaf or the patterning of veins or the leaf shape that makes them worth considering. The largest varieties will flourish in areas with mild climates, but there is no shortage of suitable species for any area with a suitably lime-free soil.

FLOWERING AND FRUITING PLANTS WITH AUTUMN COLOUR

The quality of autumn colour depends on where you garden: it is much better in regions with what might be called a continental climate, where a hot summer is followed by a sharp drop in temperature in the autumn. Soil chemistry plays a part, too, with soils that are acidic and low in nitrogen producing better colour.

Many of the best sources of autumn colour are large trees, whose leaf colour is their main source of interest. There are some smaller dual-purpose species, however, including, as we have just noted, cherries (*Prunus* spp.) and hawthorn (*Crataegus* spp.), plus the serviceberry (*Amelanchier* spp.), which has attractive flowers and fruit, and likewise many *Sorbus* species. Among shrubs, the ultimate dual-purpose species are some of the dogwoods (*Cornus* spp.), such as flowering dogwood (*C. florida*) and mountain dogwood (*C. nuttallii*), with their spectacular late-spring displays of flower and rich pink autumn colour. More reliable in a wider range of gardens than the dogwoods are euonymus, which have very good colour and bright pink and orange fruit.

THE JOYS OF YOUNG GROWTH

Young growth in spring is often an attractive feature of a plant, although it has to be said it is usually a short-lived attribute. The strong red of peonies (*Paeonia* spp.) as they emerge is very striking and is worth combining with the deep blue of lungwort (*Pulmonaria* spp.) or navelwort (*Omphalodes* spp.) for a powerful combination. Grow bluebells (*Hyacinthoides* spp.) with the shrubby *Aesculus parviflora*, a relative of the horsechestnut, for a similar reason.

Some plants are recognized for maintaining a strong coloration for a comparatively long period, sometimes up to two or three months. Varieties of *Pieris*, for example – suitable for acid soils only – combine very red young leaves with white lily-of-the-valley-type flowers in late spring, while the more vigorously growing and lime-tolerant photinias perform similarly, although their clusters of cream flowers are much less noticeable.

ORNAMENTAL GRASSES

Ornamental grasses are becoming steadily more popular, as gardeners increasingly recognize their long season of interest, which more than makes up for their lack of conventionally bright colour. Even those without coloured leaves (see pages 35–7) are useful for developing a sense of continuity. Many have attractive flower- and seedheads, which start to show in midsummer in most cases and look good until well into the winter. The majority are very weather resistant, and they are perhaps the main source of potential interest in the garden in early winter, which is the period of the year most deprived of colour.

It is perhaps unfortunate that ornamental grasses have rather a bad name with many gardeners. Not only do they not 'flower', a cardinal sin in the eyes of many, they also 'run' and take over your whole garden while you are not looking! As is so often the case in gardening, this latter myth is the result of the misbehaviour of a small number of varieties giving the rest a bad name. One of the most notable offenders in this regard is gardener's garters (*Phalaris arundinacea* 'Picta'), an attractively variegated grass that spreads like wildfire especially in damp ground. A further reason to dislike grasses is pampas grass (*Cortaderia selloana*), a majestic plant in the right place, but overplanted by unimaginative landscape contractors around industrial estates and in situations too small for it, such as the gardens of suburban bungalows. It is one of those plants that just has to have space to look good. Fortunately, most ornamental grasses are a lot smaller and much easier to place, and simpler to get rid of than either gardener's garters or pampas grass if you should tire of them.

The success of pampas grass does highlight one of the aspects of the appeal of ornamental grasses: their architectural stature. We have already noted (see page 50) how some species – *Miscanthus*, for instance – are immensely useful as architectural plants for at least half the year. Many more grasses, and the related sedges (*Carex* spp.), also have this appeal but are suited to more intimate spaces. Pendulous sedge (*Carex pendula*), with its pendant catkin-like flower- and seedheads, is a very good example of a smaller grass-like plant that has a long season of structural interest.

As well as foliage colour and architectural value, there is a third part of the long-season appeal of grasses: texture, often combined with a particular foliage colour. Now that a much more natural style of gardening is becoming popular, ornamental grasses are seen as a very important part of plant selection. After all, most open and sunny natural habitats in the temperate world are dominated by grasses. Their soft visual texture and the way they wave in the breeze are part of the appeal of fields of wildflowers, the American prairies, reed-filled marshes and alpine meadows. Getting this long season of soft naturalistic texture into the border and other plantings has become a priority for many gardeners. Grasses are more important than any other group of plants for achieving this effect.

It is important to choose the right grass for the right place, however, matching the scale of the grass species with that of the other plants in the scheme and also not cramping whatever architectural features the grass may have. For example, the two bolt upright varieties of *Calamagrostis*, *C. × acutiflora* and *C. × a.* 'Karl Foerster' (syn. *C. stricta*), look stunning on their own surrounded by lower growing plants, but they lose their impact entirely when hemmed in by other plants of equal height, whether shrubs or perennials. On the other hand, those grasses like switch grass (*Panicum virgatum*), whose charm lies in its open panicles of seed, which create a wonderfully ethereal effect, and in its autumn colour, can be happily mixed in with other perennials of the same size.

While the larger grasses contribute texture to plantings of the larger perennials or to groups of shrubs, there are many smaller ones that can do likewise to groupings of lower growing plants. This kind of planting is more conventionally 'neat' than that created by the use of large perennials and grasses. While it is the flower- and seedheads and the stems which carry them that are the source of the appeal of the larger grasses, it is the foliage of the smaller ones that makes them so useful. Hakone grass (*Hakonechloa macra*), with both green- and yellow-flushed forms, develops into a neat, softly textured mound of leaves and stems, which tend to look as if they have all been brushed one way. The brown-leaved bronze form of *Carex comans* has long, fine leaves growing in tufts. These and many others are neatly growing and so fit in well with small perennials, heathers, dwarf shrubs and conifers, and add a quality of softness that these other plant categories almost entirely lack. Since the vast majority of these grasses are evergreen, this can be a year-long aspect.

Continuity Through Planting

Efficient use of space in the garden can do much to ensure continuity of interest. The aim is to use the same space twice, by having one species following on where another has left off. The traditional way of doing this was the 'bedding out' system, whereby winter-flowering plants, such as pansies and polyanthus along with bulbs, filled beds for half the year while brightly coloured annuals took their place for the other half. Most gardeners today prefer to do this only in small patches, among more permanent planting. Here are some suggestions for other ways of utilizing space most effectively.

BULBS

Bulbs can be grown under deciduous trees and shrubs and around the crowns of summer-flowering perennials. In the border, those that flower early and leave relatively light foliage that dies back quickly are preferable – crocus and snowdrops (*Galanthus* spp.), for example. Narcissi and daffodils that leave heavier, longer lasting foliage, which can look scruffy, after flowering are more suitable for dot planting in borders or under trees.

EARLY-FLOWERING PERENNIALS

Plants such as lungwort (*Pulmonaria* spp.) and deadnettles (*Lamium* spp.) flourish under deciduous trees and shrubs. Some varieties have most attractive silver-variegated foliage, which looks good all through the summer. Hellebores have fine leaves too, which look good in borders.

SUMMER-FLOWERING CLIMBERS

Plant light summer-flowering climbers to grow over spring-flowering shrubs with dull foliage. Smaller clematis varieties, such as *C. texensis* or *C. viticella*, are suitable, or annual or half-hardy climbers such as the Chilean glory vine (*Eccremocarpus* spp.) or the cup-and-saucer vine

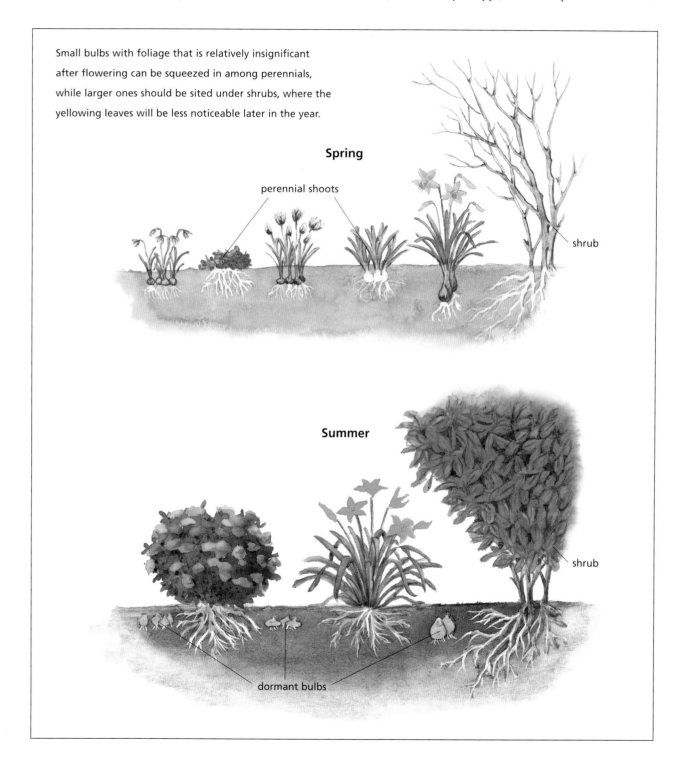

Small bulbs with foliage that is relatively insignificant after flowering can be squeezed in among perennials, while larger ones should be sited under shrubs, where the yellowing leaves will be less noticeable later in the year.

Spring

perennial shoots

shrub

Summer

shrub

dormant bulbs

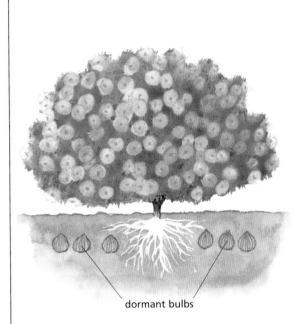

dormant bulbs

Vigorously growing and spreading summer-flowering half-hardy perennials can be planted to cover the sites of spring-flowering bulbs with little risk of disturbing them.

dormant bulbs

Hardy annuals may be sown over more deeply buried bulbs; only the surface of the soil is cultivated to avoid disturbing the dormant bulbs.

(*Cobaea* spp.). If hardy species, such as clematis, are used, they need to be ones that can be pruned to near ground level in winter, if you do not want the shrub to disappear!

COTTAGE-GARDEN ANNUALS

Old-fashioned cottage-garden annuals – love-in-the-mist (*Nigella* spp.) and pot marigolds (*Calendula officinalis*), for example – are very useful for filling in gaps in the summer border, and they are easily started from seed sown *in situ* in spring. Some, especially the two mentioned above, will very often self-sow year after year. Most can be sown in areas left bare by the annual retreat underground of spring bulbs, although it is important the bulb foliage is not cleared away until it is well yellowed.

TENDER PLANTS

Late summer- and autumn-flowering tender plants – such as osteospermum, diascia and marguerites (*Argyranthemum*) – can be used to great effect in borders. Grow them in the gaps between earlier flowering plants or to cover ground occupied by spring-flowering bulbs. Their speed of growth, more often sideways than upwards, and free-flowering nature make them ideal for high-speed summer space filling.

CONTAINERS

Containers of flowering plants can be used in and around borders if there is no space for more planting or an instant effect is wanted. You can make a feature of the container, or you can hide it among other plants. See the chapter on Containers for more ideas on using plants in this way.

Early-flowering Perennials

It is helpful to be aware that certain perennials go dormant by the middle of the summer, including *Papaver orientale*, species of *Crambe* and *Gypsophila paniculata*, and, if they are grown in shade, species of *Dicentra* and *Polygonatum*. In other words, you may be left with an embarrassing gap. Good planning will ensure that there will be something else in front ready to take over for the rest of the summer.

LATE-FLOWERING PERENNIALS

There are a few mid- and late summer-flowering perennials whose habit of growth is so wispy that they are almost transparent; they do not shade surrounding plants and it is possible to see past their fine stems. The violet-flowered South American vervain (*Verbena bonariensis*; syn. *V. patagonica*) and white-flowered *Gaura lindheimeri* are two, the grass golden oats (*Stipa gigantea*) is another. They are very effective when combined with earlier flowering, low-growing plants, such as winter heathers or creeping rockery-type plants.

AUTUMN-FLOWERING BULBS

This is an often-underestimated group of plants. *Cyclamen hederifolium* is very successful in the dry shade beneath trees and shrubs. There are also autumn-flowering crocuses and colchicums, although the latter have spring foliage, which takes up an amount of space out of all proportion to the size of the flowers. Nerines and belladonna lilies (*Amaryllis belladonna*) are also autumn flowering and love (and only really flourish in) hot, dry places at the foot of walls.

SHADE-LOVING PLANTS

Late-flowering shade-loving plants are really few and far between, so you should make the most of *Aster divaricatus*, *A. macrophyllus* and white snakeroot (*Eupatorium rugosum*), which are all white flowered and grow well at the edge of tree and shrub canopies, lighting up the shade. Such later developers can be blended with the more numerous spring-flowering shade plants. They also make suitable companions for foxgloves, which are turning to seed by the time they flower.

WINTER INTEREST

Too many gardeners give up in despair at the idea of making their garden interesting in winter, retreating indoors to mull through seed catalogues by the fire. Few of these

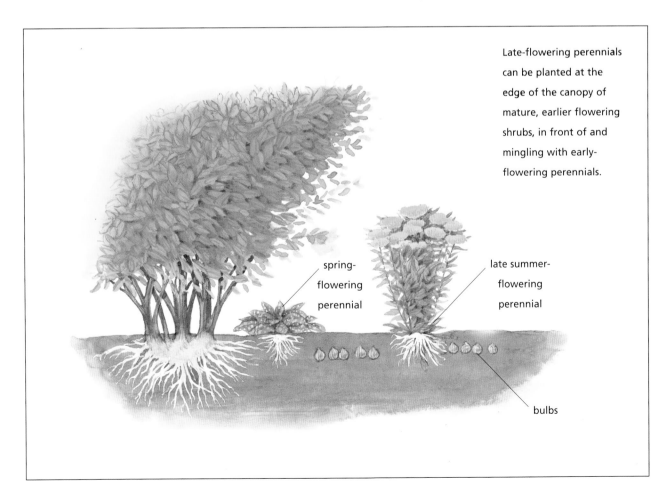

Late-flowering perennials can be planted at the edge of the canopy of mature, earlier flowering shrubs, in front of and mingling with early-flowering perennials.

spring-flowering perennial

late summer-flowering perennial

bulbs

fair-weather gardeners may be enticed out further than the nearest clump of rain-spattered hellebores, although real enthusiasts wax lyrical about these flowers, and snowdrops (*Galanthus* spp.) have their devotees. One snowdrop may look much like another to most of us, but to some (known as galanthophiles), there are innumerable subtly different cultivars.

Even a gardener who is unwilling to set foot in the garden during winter still has to look at it through the windows, however, so there is a strong argument for at least making an attempt. So, what alternatives to evergreens are there?

The key to much effective winter planting is to make use of the warm-toned, low winter light. Leaving perennials uncut, so that the sun can illuminate the myriad shades of brown of their dead stems, is definitely more rewarding than 'tidying them all up' so that the sun has nothing to shine on except bare earth and a few sticks. Ornamental grasses, as we have already noted, are particularly effective at this season.

Some trees and shrubs have highly ornamental bark, the birches (*Betula* spp.), cherries (*Prunus* spp.), dogwoods (*Cornus* spp.) and willows (*Salix* spp.) being especially good. The bark of the young growth of some willows – *Salix alba* subsp. *vitellina*, for example – can be quite spectacular when the sun hits it, making it a glowing orange-brown. Others have purple-tinged or red-tinged twigs. So, if space allows, much can be made of willow and dogwood, both of which need to be cut down regularly to ground level (every two years) so that there is plenty of young growth. With birches and cherries, it is the trunk rather than the twigs that are the most attractive features.

Most winter flowers require close examination to be appreciated fully, which means that they benefit from planting somewhere where they can be seen without you getting too muddy. *Clematis cirrhosa*, with its purple-spotted yellow flowers, could be close to the front door, and witch hazel (*Hamamelis* spp.), which produces the most bewitching scent from its tiny flowers, needs to be sited near a path, too.

Cotoneaster berries provide some vivid winter colour, while the *Helleborus foetidus* below will flower as the berries disappear.

Making a Garden Calendar and Lengthening Seasonal Interest

A garden calendar consists simply of a table that lists varieties down one side and times of year along the top. It enables you to see at a glance what is flowering or looking good when, especially if colours are used. The calendar enables the gardener to plan to improve the planting and to work out colour combinations for different times of year.

The illustration shows an example of the kind of planting that is often found in gardens that have received little attention for some years. There is some spring and early-summer interest and then something of a gap until late summer. There is only room for a row of one or two perennials in front of the shrubs.

Additional new plants are chosen to give a greatly enhanced seasonal spread, with some of the large old clumps of perennials removed or thinned out. Some pruning of the established shrubs is carried out to restrict their size.

The revamped planting is shown in early and late summer. New plants are indicated with an asterisk (*). Evergreens are indicated by a continuous line, and decorative seedheads by a dark line. Continued intermittent or low-level flowering after the main season, as with the geranium, is indicated by a broken line.

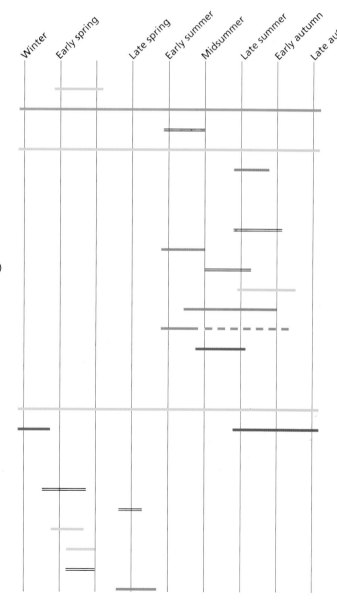

Shrubs

1 .*Forsythia* x *intermedia*

2. *Prunus laurocerasus*

3. *Philadelphus* 'Virginal'

4. *Thuja plicata* 'Collyer's Gold'

F.*Caryopteris* x *clandonensis* 'Kew Blue'

Perennials

5. *Aster* (white variety)

6. *Geranium* x *magnificum*

7. *Leucanthemum* x *superbum* (syn. *Chrysanthemum* x *superbum*)

8. *Solidago* (variety)

B.* *Aster* x *frikartii* 'Mönch'

A.* *Geranium* x *oxonianum* 'Winscombe'

D.* *Monarda* 'Capricorn'

Grasses

E.* *Carex testacea*

C.* *Miscanthus sinensis* 'Kleine Silberspinne'

Bulbs

9. *Galanthus nivalis*

10. *Narcissus* 'Actaea'

* *Crocus chrysanthus* (varieties)

* *Narcissus* 'February Gold'

* *Narcissus* 'February Silver'

* *Hyacinthoides hispanica*

Before – late summer

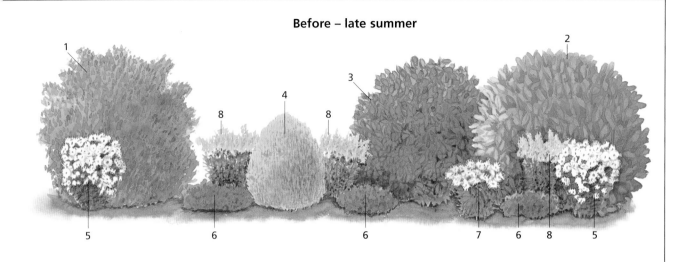

After – early summer

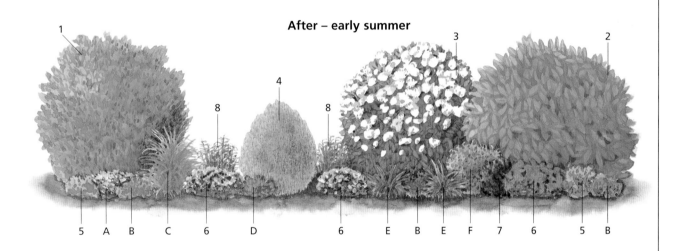

After – late summer

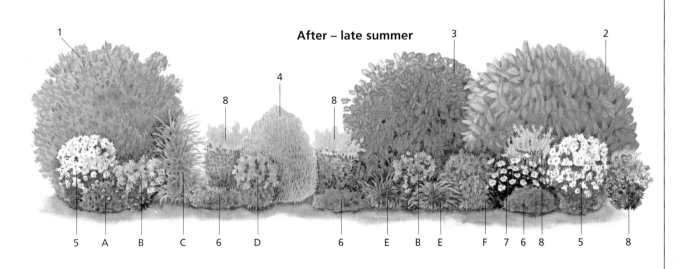

Plant Directory

Reliable Spring Colour

Bulbs, such as snowdrops (*Galanthus* spp.), crocuses, daffodils (*Narcissus* spp.) and scillas, are most people's first choice of reliable spring colour. The following is a selection of the best, long-lived non-bulb options.

Caltha palustris
(marsh marigold, kingcup)

- Clump-forming herbaceous perennial
- 30 x 40cm (12 x 16in)
- Striking yellow buttercup-shaped flowers in early spring are borne on a plant that loves really wet places – pond edges or marsh, for example – but which will grow in ordinary garden conditions if it is not too dry.
- Plant in a position in full sun.

Corydalis flexuosa

- Spreading herbaceous perennial
- 15 x 30cm (6 x 12in)
- The electric blue flowers, appearing in mid-spring, are a real eye-catcher – and to think that this plant was unknown in cultivation only a decade or so ago! It has attractive feathery foliage, too. A good choice to accompany yellows.
- Plant in shade and in well-drained, moist soil.

Daphne mezereum
(mezereon)

- Deciduous shrub
- 1 x 1m (3 x 3ft)
- Purple-pink flowers with a delicious scent hug the leafless branches in late winter. *D. m.* f. *alba* is a rather lovely white form. This plant can be relatively short lived.
- Plant in full sun or very light shade, in any well-drained soil that is, preferably, alkaline.

Omphalodes cappadocica

- Slowly spreading herbaceous perennial
- 20 x 30cm (8 x 12in)
- Exquisite blue flowers are the distinguishing mark of this low-growing, ground-covering shade-lover. It needs fairly quiet companions if it is to be appreciated – lungwort (*Pulmonaria* spp.) and lily-of-the-valley (*Convallaria* spp.) perhaps.
- Plant in any well-drained but reasonably moist soil.

Pulmonaria
(lungwort)

- Slowly spreading, clump-forming, semi-evergreen perennials
- 20 x 40cm (8 x 16in)
- Deep, clear blue flowers mark out *P. angustifolia*. There are now lots of varieties available, with flowers in a range of pinks and blues, and some with attractive silver-splashed foliage, *P. saccharata* 'Leopard' being the best of these.
- Ideally, plant in light shade, in a well-drained but moist soil.

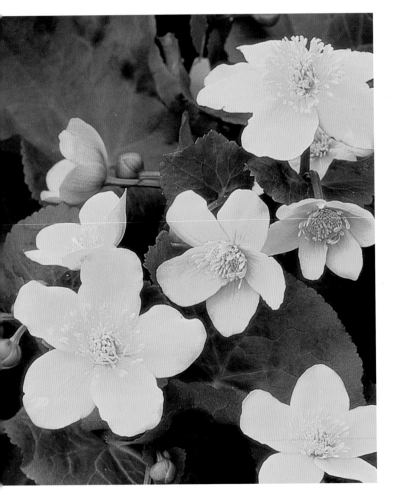

Caltha palustris

Long-lasting Summer Colour

It often surprises people how few plants actually flower all summer long. From the plants' point of view, such length of flowering would, perhaps, be rather too much to expect. Annuals and short-lived perennials tend to be among the most reliable.

Calendula officinalis
(pot marigold)

- Annual
- 30 x 30cm (12 x 12in)
- This is the true marigold, not those ill-proportioned things (*Tagetes*) that look like a child's drawing of a flower. This marigold has flowers in shades of yellow and orange, with a real summery daisy smell, that go on from early summer until midwinter, if the weather is mild. They often self-sow, too.
- Grow in sun and in any reasonable soil.

Erysimum
'Bowles Mauve'
(wallflower)

- Short-lived evergreen perennial
- 60 x 60cm (24 x 24in)
- Smothered with rich lavender-mauve flowers from mid-spring until midsummer, this perennial wallflower is a wonderful addition to early summer pastel flower schemes or cottage-garden borders. It is easy to propagate from cuttings, which is fortunate as it rarely performs well for more than two years.
- Plant in sun and in any reasonable soil.

Lavatera 'Rosea'

- Short-lived evergreen shrub
- 2 x 3m (6 x 10ft)
- This might be better for the chapter on 'Instant' Gardens, as it grows enormous, at terrific speed, and is smothered with large, deep pink flowers all summer long, but then only lives a few years. L. 'Barnsley', a pink-white bicolour, is more subtle.
- Plant in sun and in any soil that is not waterlogged.

Osteospermum

- Evergreen perennials of varying habit
- Covered with big daisy-like flowers all summer, these are very good value. *O. jucundum*, 30 x 50cm (12 x 20in), is hardy in most sunny places; it has pinkish-white flowers and a densely creeping habit. *O.* 'Buttermilk' is more upright, 60 x 50cm (24 x 20in), with lovely soft yellow flowers. There are many others, white-, pink- or blue-stained, few of which are reliably hardy but which make first-class summer specials.
- Plant in full sun and in any reasonable soil.

Verbena bonariensis
(syn. *V. patagonica*; South American vervain)

- Short-lived herbaceous perennial
- 1.5 x 0.3m (5 x 1ft)
- Purple flowers on a slender, almost leafless stem make this a 'transparent' plant – that is, you can see through its haze of flowers to whatever is growing behind. Butterflies love it. It usually survives the winter but nearly always self-seeds anyway, which is another part of its charm.
- Plant in full sun and in any reasonable soil, although it will grow in poor and dry soils.

Late-summer and Autumn Colour

This is not a difficult time to fill the garden with colour, whatever some may say. Late-flowering members of the daisy family keep going a surprisingly long time before giving way to the russet tones of dying leaves and winter berries.

Euonymus europaeus 'Red Cascade'

Acer palmatum

(Japanese maple)

- Deciduous tree
- 5 x 5m (16 x 16ft) ultimately
- The classic Japanese maple, with the most stunning autumn colour of all. There is a large number of different varieties available. *A. p.* 'Osakazuki' has scarlet autumn leaves. *A. p.* Dissectum Atropurpureum Group is one of the miniatures, 1.5 x 2m (5 x 6ft), with finely divided leaves that are purple all summer, turning orange when autumn arrives.
- Light shade, a moist but well-drained soil and protection from winds are essential.

Aster x *frikartii* 'Mönch'

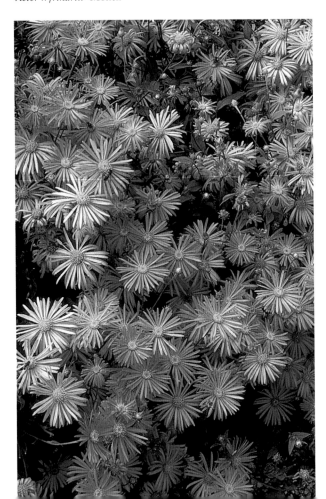

Aster

(Michaelmas daisy, starwort)

- Slowly spreading, clump-forming herbaceous perennial
- Varieties mentioned are 100 x 40cm (36 x 16in), which is pretty average for the genus
- A vast number of asters is available for late-season colour. Many are put off by the mildew that the old-fashioned Michaelmas daisies get, but this must not be held against them, as the vast majority are immune. *A.* 'Little Carlow' (*cordifolius* hybrid), with fine blue flowers in sprays, and *A.* x *frikartii* 'Mönch', with larger blue flowers, are the best.
- Grow in sun or very light shade and in any reasonable soil that does not dry out.

Enkianthus

- Deciduous small trees
- 3 x 3m (10 x 10ft)
- Vivid scarlet autumn colour and lily-of-the-valley-type flowers are two reasons for growing these compact, small-growing trees. *E. campanulatus* is the most widely available.
- Plant in light shade. Moist but well-drained acid soil is essential.

Euonymus

(spindle tree)

- Deciduous small trees and shrubs
- The autumn colour is often not reliable, but the deciduous euonymus are among the best and least fussy of plants, and small enough for most gardens. *E. alatus* (winged spindle tree) is pink-red and reaches 2 x 4m (6 x 13ft). *E. europaeus* is 4 x 6m (13 x 20ft) and has startling pink and orange fruit.
- Plant in sun or light shade and in any reasonable soil, preferably one that is alkaline.

Schizostylis coccinea

- Slowly spreading, clump-forming perennial
- 60 x 30cm (24 x 12in)
- Small spikes of red flowers are borne among long, narrow leaves from early autumn until the first frosts. The variety *S. c.* 'Mrs Hegarty' has delicate pink flowers.
- Although it does best in mild maritime climates, it is reasonably hardy if sensibly placed. Plant in sun and in a moist soil.

Further suggestions

Amelanchier spp. (serviceberry); *Callicarpa* spp.; *Ceratostigma* spp.; *Colchicum* spp. (autumn crocus); *Crocosmia* spp.; *Cyclamen hederifolium*; *Hebe* 'Midsummer Beauty'; *Liquidambar* spp.; *Nerine* spp.; *Penstemon* spp. (beard-tongue); *Phygelius* spp.; *Physalis alkekengi* (bladder cherry, winter cherry); *Pyracantha* spp.; *Rhus* spp. (sumac); *Rudbeckia* spp.; *Salvia* (sage) late-flowering species and varieties; *Solidago* spp. (golden rod); *Sorbus* spp. (rowan); *Stewartia* spp.; *Vernonia* spp.

Winter Colour

Winter flowers tend to be subtle, and they often need close inspection to be appreciated. One wonders rather cynically whether anybody would get excited about the following if they flowered in midsummer.

Clematis cirrhosa

- Deciduous climber
- 3 x 3m (10 x 10ft)
- Palest cream-yellow flowers are spotted with purple. This is a good plant to have climbing around the door.
- Plant in sun and in any reasonable soil. It is hardy in most areas, but keep it out of wind and frost pockets.

Hamamelis
(witch hazel)

- Deciduous shrubs
- 5 x 6m (16 x 20ft) ultimately
- The numerous varieties of *H.* x *intermedia* are distinguished by their small, russet-toned flowers, which have a most exquisite smell.
- Plant in light shade. Well-drained moist, preferably acid, soil is essential for this slow-growing plant.

Helleborus foetidus
(stinking hellebore)

- Evergreen perennial
- 60 x 50cm (24 x 20in)
- A truly stately plant, with elegantly poised, hand-shaped dark leaves and green flowers, which emerge slowly to flower in late winter. *H. f.* Wester Flisk Group has finer and even more elegant leaves. Somewhat short lived, it comes readily from seed and often self-sows.
- Plant in light shade and in any reasonable soil. It will tolerate dry shade to some extent.

Helleborus orientalis
(Lenten rose)

- Clump-forming perennial
- 40 x 40cm (16 x 16in)
- The source of some of the most fashionable (and expensive) plants of recent years, with maroon-blacks, yellows and extensive spotting being the sought-after characteristics among a wide range of (not very bright) colours. Flowering from late winter to mid-spring, these hellebores are quite special, but I do wish they would point their faces to the onlooker and not look bashfully at the mud.
- Plant in sun or light shade and in any soil that does not dry out.

Salix alba subsp. *vitellina*
'Britzensis'
(syn. *S. alba* 'Chermesina')

- Deciduous tree
- 10 x 6m (33 x 20ft) if not cut back
- Glowing orange in the winter light, the twigs of this willow are a beautiful backdrop to the garden. Only young growth shows this colour, so annual or biennial cutting back to the ground is vital (it's a good idea anyway, unless you have a park to fill).

Further suggestions

Chimonanthus praecox (wintersweet); *Cornus alba* (red-barked dogwood); *Correa* 'Mannii' (syn. *C.* 'Harrisii'); *Cyclamen coum*; *Erica carnea*; *Iris unguicularis* (syn. *I. stylosa*; Algerian iris); *Lonicera* x *purpusii*; *Mahonia* x *media* 'Charity'; *Prunus* x *subhirtella* (higan cherry); *Viburnum* x *bodnantense*

The scented dimension

So far, we have only considered plants in visual terms. Scent is a quality that enables us to add another entire dimension to our gardening – truly a major potential transformation. Unlike the visual appearance of plants, which is so largely relative, scent is generally appreciated in absolute terms. Up to now, we have been considering plant colours and textures in relation to each other to a great extent, but scents are nearly always experienced on their own. The only way that we can compare them is to take in each sequentially, one after another, which is quite a different experience from viewing a border full of plants in a continuous sweep.

Fragrance is the term applied to floral scents, which exist in order to advertise the presence of the flower to insects, to entice them to come and feed off the nectar and be tricked into fertilizing it. Aromatic is the word used to describe the different range of scents that are emitted when the leaves of certain plants are crushed or heated, forcing them to release various oils.

Scents are difficult to characterize, to remember or to describe. Perhaps this is part of the reason why scent seems to be so little regarded by plant breeders. Modern roses are notorious for having no scent – or, more accurately, little scent – compared with older varieties. And yet our nineteenth-century ancestors obviously rated scent most highly, as their favourite plants were nearly always fragrant. It seems that today many people often do not even consider fragrance. It is a constant surprise frequently to come across plants with a distinct fragrance

Above: *Lilium regale* has one of the most sumptious scents of any garden plant. It grows well in large containers, too.

that is never mentioned in their entries in reference books.

It is therefore not unexpected that selecting plants for fragrance involves entering uncharted waters. It is worthwhile having a sniff of every new flower you come across, as the chances are that this is the only way you will find out if it has any fragrance or if you like it. Different cultivars of the same species will often have marked differences in the quality and intensity of their scent, which makes it vital that if you are particularly interested in developing this aspect of the garden you experiment with a variety before you buy it.

Using Fragrance in the Garden

Remarkably few gardens are developed that put fragrance centre stage. It should be possible to design a garden that presents the visitor with a whole series of scented experiences as they walk around, depending on the season. The fragrances of most temperate plants need to be taken in by getting right up close to the flower and smelling it, which does certainly limit or constrain one's progress

around the garden. There are, however, certain plants that emit a strong enough fragrance for it to waft through the air, so that they can be smelt several metres downwind. These are mostly plants whose aim is to attract evening- or night-flying moths and other insects (and, not surprisingly, they tend to have white or pale flowers), such as jasmines or philadelphus.

Scent is easily blown away, which makes the location of scented plants whose fragrance wafts in this way very important. Sheltered corners of gardens are vital if the breeze is not to carry the scent away. Proximity to somewhere where the scent is likely to be experienced is important too – near a path or a sitting area, perhaps. Scented climbers can best be appreciated if they are encouraged to climb around windows which are frequently opened, or near to doors.

Those flowers – the vast majority – which can be smelled only close to present more of a problem when it comes to displaying them. Primroses smell sweet, but who regularly gets down on their hands and knees in late winter to sample the scent? Raised beds, window boxes and containers that can be lifted or placed in a more accessible position or even raised beds or rockeries are all useful means of bringing flowers nearer to our noses.

Herb gardens offer the opportunity to bring together a wide variety of aromatic foliage plants; summer evenings will meld their scents into one intoxicating whole.

Using Aromatic Foliage

Aromatic foliage is a more immediately rewarding quality to work with than flower scent, for the same reasons that foliage interest has certain advantages over floral – its longer season. Most plants with aromatic foliage come from Mediterranean-type climates, where the aromatic oils are part of the plants' defence against water loss in the hot summer sun. Many are herbs, culinary or medicinal. It follows that most will need a sunny planting site, which will also encourage the production of scent on warm days.

Apart from warm, still days, the best way to experience aromatic foliage is to release it by slightly bruising the leaves, either by walking on the plants, rubbing the leaves or in some cases by simply brushing past them. Camomile (*Chamaemelum nobile*; syn. *Anthemis nobilis*) and creeping thymes (*Thymus* spp.) can be grown as ground cover or among paving stones, where they will be stepped on, or they can be included as part of stone or turf seats. Larger aromatic plants need to be within handling distance, grown along paths or in raised beds.

Given the common ground between culinary herbs and aromatic-leaved plants, it is not surprising that the two are often combined. The proximity of herb gardens to the kitchen also means they are close to the house and thus close to appreciation.

Fragrance Through the Seasons

A sunny day in winter, which encourages the production and spread of scent, can be surprising, chiefly because of the witch hazels (*Hamamelis* spp.), whose strange little russet-toned flowers emit a bewitching and potentially far-reaching fragrance that is at least as good as any to be experienced in summer. In addition, there are a number of flowering shrubs with inconspicuous but well-scented flowers – wintersweet (*Chimonanthus praecox*) and the honeysuckle relative *Lonicera* × *purpusii*, for example. Both are best trained as wall shrubs in gardens where space is limited and perhaps regarded primarily as a source of cutting material for floral displays inside the house. The somewhat more showy viburnums, such as *Viburnum fragrans*, are worth growing as naturally formed bushes.

Daphnes are slow-growing shrubs, whose compact size makes them useful for small gardens and raised beds and

Old-fashioned roses underplanted with herbs means that two very different kinds of fragrance can be experienced in proximity.

whose scent is quite incomparable. *D. mezereum* bears its strong pink flowers on leafless branches, whereas the others are mostly white flowered and evergreen. All daphnes need a soil that does not dry out, but one that is well drained and preferably alkaline. Once planted, they should never be disturbed.

Many bulbs and low-growing perennials have good spring-time scents, but, as we have noted, they are not the easiest to appreciate. Two in particular were popular in Victorian times as pot plants – the sweet violet (*Viola odorata*) and lily-of-the-valley (*Convallaria majalis*) – and these were 'forced' – that is, brought indoors in pots to flower.

Shrubs are the main source of scented interest from midwinter through to midsummer. Some, such as varieties of philadelphus, known as mock orange for its resemblance to the scent of orange blossom, are infamously large growers, needing careful placing in the garden or to be grown trained to a wall and pruned just after flowering every year to limit their growth. Deciduous azaleas – that is, *Rhododendron luteum* (azalea species) – and most of the Mollis and Ghent hybrids have a superb, strong and utterly sensuous scent. Those who garden on alkaline soils and who cannot grow them can enjoy almost the same experience from the lime-tolerant *Viburnum carlesii* or *V. × carlcephalum*.

From early summer on, it is roses that are perhaps the mainstay of the fragrant garden. Varieties should be carefully chosen, not only because many are poorly scented, but also because of those that are well scented, there is an enormous variation between cultivars. This is one of the special aspects of roses, the way that in the manner of a human bee, one can move from flower to flower and experience completely different fragrances, yet all are recognizable as roses. I am sure that there is someone somewhere in the world who can distinguish between roses on the basis of scent alone.

In addition, there are the moss roses, old varieties that have a mossy growth around the buds, which have a deep and resinous scent. Then there is the incense rose (*Rosa primula*), whose foliage is strongly scented of incense – an aroma which, on a still summer evening, can be carried a surprisingly long distance.

The fragrance of honeysuckle (*Lonicera* spp.) is the other classic garden scent in early and midsummer. Vigorous climbers, honeysuckles need plenty of space and are ideal for covering walls and fences, perhaps grown in conjunction with climbing roses and wisteria, which is also scented. All cultivars of the common *L. periclymenum* are strongly fragrant, but not all of the other species are scented.

Midsummer onwards sees a definite diminution in the number of fragrant flowers in the garden. The scent of the late-flowering members of the daisy family, which so dominate late summer and autumn, is by no means absent, but it is nothing to get carried away with. Lilies are useful for early to midsummer, and if started late in pots they can be the mainstay of the fragrant garden in summer. Regal lily (*Lilium regale*), with its large white flowers, certainly has one of the richest fragrances of any hardy plant and one that carries well too. Perhaps half-hardy plants should be regarded as the main source of later season scent.

Using Half-hardy Scented Plants

Certain subtropical plants can be grown in containers or bedded out for the summer to provide us with either fragrant flowers or a wider range of aromatic foliage. Heliotrope (*Heliotropum arborescens*; syn. *H. peruvianum*) is an old Victorian favourite which has recently seen a resurgence in popularity, whose deep violet flowers, borne all summer long, have a beautifully rich scent.

Verbena 'Pink Parfait' is a new cultivar of a recently popular plant, the trailing verbenas that combine so well with petunias, pelargoniums and other summer container plants. Its apricot-pink flowers have the most bewitching warm and full fragrance. Daturas (*Brugmansia* spp.) are often used as summer specimen plants, but their night-time fragrance is quite unforgettable – the quintessence of the tropics.

While there is a wide variety of hardy plants with aromatic leaves, the selection can be made more exciting by the addition of half-hardy species, notably scented-leaf pelargoniums and salvias.

The pelargoniums can be kept in containers, combined with other summer species or planted out in beds or borders. A particularly successful herb garden I know includes them with culinary herbs and other hardy aromatics in a sheltered corner of a walled garden. On a summer evening their different scents rise up and mingle to fill the surrounding air.

While the aromatic-leaved salvias, all closely related to the culinary sage, can be appreciated all summer long, they are at their best in late summer and autumn, when they have grown into substantial bushy plants and are drawing attention to themselves with their brightly coloured flowers. Like the pelargoniums, each has a distinct aroma of its own, that of the pineapple sage (*Salvia elegans* 'Scarlet Pineapple'; syn. *S. rutilans*) being easily the most distinctive. Being vigorous growers, they do much better when they are planted out in a border than when grown in pots, and they can then be taken up for the winter and housed in a frost-free place.

Several other half-hardy aromatic plants seem ideal for growing in containers and placing around a seating area. Lemon verbena (*Aloysia triphylla*; syn. *A. citriodora*) is well known, although the Australian mint-bushes (*Prostanthera* spp.) are less so. Even in a confined space, it is possible to grow a wide range of hardy aromatic plants in containers, most of them adapting well to slight root restriction.

Plant Directory

Scented Flowers

A garden without scent is truly lacking a dimension. The following are among the most highly rated of many worthwhile plants.

Convallaria majalis
(lily-of-the-valley)

- Spreading tuberous perennial
- 15 x 20cm (6 x 8in)
- The white flowers have a rich, refined scent in spring. Once established, they will spread strongly. Lilies-of-the-valley can be grown in pots and brought into the house in late winter for better appreciation of their scent.
- Plant, preferably, in fertile, moist but well-drained soil in shade.

Heliotropum arborescens
(syn. *H. peruvianum*; heliotrope)

- Evergreen shrub
- 60 x 60cm (24 x 24in) when grown as an annual
- Flowers in shades of purple with a fulsome scent are borne throughout the summer. Heliotrope can be grown as an annual, planted out after the last frosts and discarded at the end of the year, or dug up and overwintered in a greenhouse.
- Plant in sun and in fertile soil.

Convallaria majalis

Lilium regale
(regal lily)

• Bulb

• 100 x 30cm (36 x 12in)

• The large, creamy-white trumpet flowers appear in summer and have a fantastic fragrance.

• Plant in sun and in fertile, moist but well-drained soil. Alternatively, they can be grown in pots and dotted around seating areas.

Osmanthus delavayi

• Evergreen shrub

• 3 x 3m (10 x 10ft)

• Clusters of small white, sweetly scented flowers are borne in spring. The leaves are neat and glossy.

• Plant in sun or light shade and in any reasonable soil, but avoid cold, windy sites.

Primula florindae
(giant cowslip)

• Slowly spreading herbaceous perennial

• 50 x 30cm (20 x12in)

• Yellow or orange flowers top stout stems in early to midsummer. They have a delicious, spicy fragrance, quite unlike anything else.

• Plant in sun or light shade and in any reasonable soil. They do best in moist ground or by water.

Verbena
'Pink Parfait'

• Perennial

• 20 x 30cm (8 x 12in)

• Pale pink flowers with a most beautiful scent are usually grown in hanging baskets or containers to make appreciation easier.

• Plant out in sun after the last frosts and bring in under cover or take cuttings to overwinter.

Further suggestions

Acacia dealbata (mimosa, silver wattle); *Buddleja* spp. (buddleia); *Daphne* spp.; *Brugmansia* spp. (datura); *Elaeagnus pungens*; *Erysimum* spp. (syn. *Cheiranthus* spp.; wallflower); *Magnolia* spp.; *Mahonia* spp.; *Philadelphus* (mock orange), *Phlox* spp.; *Rhododendron* deciduous 'azalea' kinds, Ghent and Mollis hybrids; *Rosa* so-called old-fashioned varieties; *Sambucus* spp. (elder); *Syringa* spp. (lilac); *Viburnum* x *bodnantense*, *V.* x *carlcephalum, V. carlesii; Viola odorata* (sweet violet); *Wisteria* spp.; practically all bulbs

Aromatic Foliage

Plants with aromatic foliage add yet another dimension to the garden. Most species that have grey leaves are aromatic, as well as a good many others, a fact often not recognized in reference books. These are simply the most spectacular.

Lilium regale

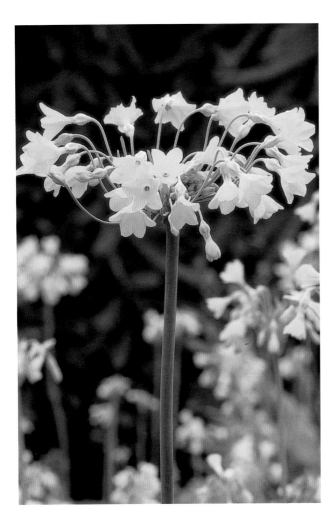

Primula florindae

Aloysia triphylla
(syn. *A. citriodora*, *Lippia citriodora*; lemon verbena)
- Deciduous shrub
- 3 x 3m (10 x 10ft), in open ground in warm climates
- A vigorous shrub with light green leaves that release a strong lemony scent when brushed. The flowers are small and white.
- Lemon verbena withstands only light frosts and should be overwintered under cover. Plant in sun.

Calomeria amaranthoides
(syn. *Humea elegans*; incense plant)
- Biennial
- 1.5 x 0.6m (5 x 2ft)
- Strongly scented of incense, this biennial has towering clusters of tiny brown-red flowers in its second year. It is rather extraordinary all round. Save seed to propagate.

Lavandula stoechas
(French lavender)
- Evergreen shrub
- 60 x 60cm (24 x 24in)
- The silvery foliage has a rich aroma, and the mauve flowers, with spectacular winged petals, are borne on thin stems.
- Plant in full sun and in any reasonable soil, including poor and dry ones. Site away from cold winds and severe frosts.

Prostanthera cuneata
(alpine mint bush)
- Evergreen shrub
- 60 x 60cm (24 x 24in)
- The leaves of this little shrub have a scent that combines incense with mint. The flowers are white.
- Grow in sun and in any reasonable soil. Avoid the coldest sites.

Salvia elegans
'Scarlet Pineapple'
(syn. *S. rutilans*; pineapple sage)
- Evergreen shrub
- 100 x 70cm (36 x 28in)
- Bright scarlet flowers light up pineapple sage in late summer and autumn. The leaves smell strongly of pineapple. Like all these late-flowering, very colourful aromatic sages, protection from frost is needed. Insulating the roots with straw will suffice in more sheltered areas, but otherwise you will need to bring it in under cover for the winter.

Further suggestions

Achillea spp. (milfoil, yarrow); *Anthemis* spp.; *Artemisia* spp. (wormwood); *Calamintha* spp. (calamint); *Eucalyptus* spp. (gum tree); *Leptospermum* spp.; *Mentha* spp. (mint); *Myrtus* spp. (myrtle); *Nepeta* spp.; *Ocimum* spp. (basil); *Origanum* spp. (marjoram, dittany); *Rosmarinus* spp. (rosemary); *Ruta* spp. (rue), *Santolina* spp. (cotton lavender); *Satureia* spp. (savory); *Teucrium* spp. (germander); *Thymus* spp. (thyme); all conifers

Shade

Shade is too often regarded as a problem. Yet it also has advantages, as many shade-loving plants are extremely attractive and are evergreen, too. Indeed, the variety of foliage colour, form and texture among shade-lovers is greater than that among sun-lovers, which helps to make up for the reduced frequency and intensity of flowers. There is one other advantage too – weeds, especially grasses, do not grow nearly as well in shady conditions.

Too often, the potential of shaded areas in the garden is unrealized. They are generally nothing more than dark, dank spaces filled with overgrown and misshapen shrubs that have long ceased to flower or masses of rampant ground cover, like ivy. A transformed shade garden, although it may not stop the traffic, can certainly give a great deal of pleasure.

Bringing life to a shaded area of the garden has to start with an understanding of what kind of shade it is that you have. There is 'light' shade, where there is sun for half the day or at least a few hours. There is 'high' shade, which is cast by the high branches of trees; 'dappled' shade is cast by a light branch canopy; 'full' shade is pretty dark; and there is 'dry' shade, the most dreaded of all, where, indeed, little will grow. The shade cast by different kinds of tree varies, too, and is often exacerbated by other factors. Beeches and maples, for example, cast a deep shade and are highly effective at taking up moisture and nutrients from the soil and, in the autumn, smothering everything underneath with a carpet of leaves that are slow to rot down. The shade cast by conifers is perhaps the most problematic, because there is no opportunity for plants

Above: Hostas, hardy geraniums and dicentras are classic plants for light shade and a reasonably moist soil.

to make use of winter sunlight. Buildings create shade too, and if there are overhanging eaves and rubble-filled borders and foundations the problem will be made worse by drought and soil poverty.

'Easy' Shade

The least problematic shade is that cast by trees on a damp and fertile soil. The ready availability of moisture and nutrients helps to make up for the lack of light, allowing many sun-loving plants to grow in light shade and many species from lightly shaded conditions to flourish well under the trees.

Moist shade is a splendid opportunity to grow lushly beautiful plants such as ferns, the plume-flowered astilbes and the colourful candelabra primulas. Such an area can easily be as cheerful as any sun-soaked border until midsummer at least. There are flowers for the rest of the summer – the big yellow ligularia daisies, with their large and distinctive foliage, for example – but they are best seen as secondary to the delights of luxuriant foliage.

Some of the most distinctive large foliage plants (see page 59) flourish best in moist shade. Not only do they have all the water they need, but the trees that cast the shade can protect them from damaging winds. The classic foliage plants for shade are hostas; there are a truly

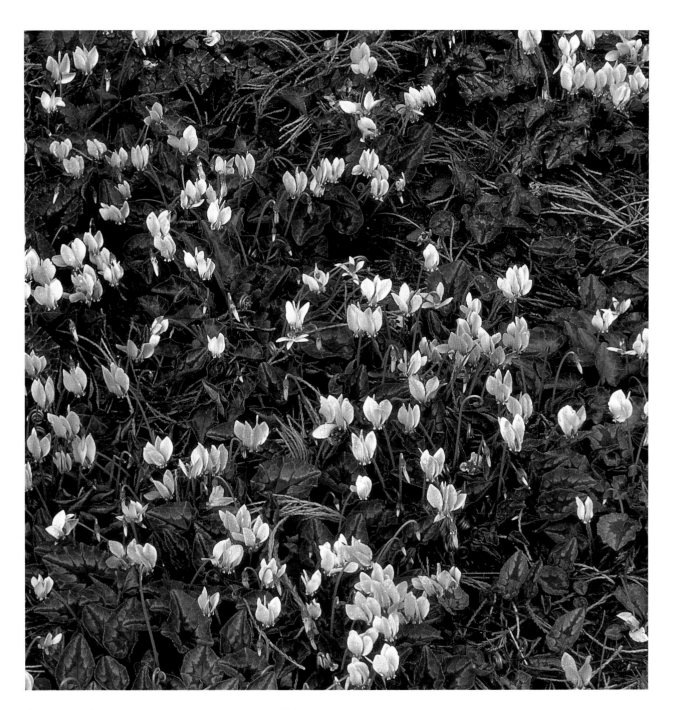

Cyclamen hederifolium is not only a charmingly beautiful plant but a robust one too, growing in the dry shade beneath trees that is all too often barren.

Moist shade provides an opportunity to create some wonderfully lush plantings; here candelabra primulas grow alongside *Meconopsis grandis*.

vast number of varieties, many with grey, gold and silver-variegated foliage. I feel they are greatly overused and monotonous *en masse*. In addition, they are not evergreen and are top of the menu for slugs, especially when the young leaves are unfurling in spring. They do look good mixed with ferns, however, which provide a contrast in texture.

The shade of deciduous trees at least allows plants to grow through the winter, which is why many woodland plants are evergreen, such as the hellebores with their clumps of hand-shaped leaves or the hart's tongue fern (*Asplenium scolopendrium*; syn. *Phyllitis scolopendrium*), with its distinctive strap-shaped leaves, which seems to be able to survive in the darkest shade.

Most woodlanders are spring flowering. Those with bulbs or tuberous roots can make a lot of growth early in the year, utilizing the previous year's stored nutrients to grow when temperatures are low. Given how rapidly bulbs, such as snowdrops (*Galanthus* spp.), and tuberous plants, such as the multi-coloured varieties of *Anemone blanda*, become established, transforming a shaded area into a successful spring garden is easy.

'Difficult' Shade

Deep shade allows only very few plants to thrive, generally those species with leathery and often dark evergreen leaves. Describing them as 'quietly beautiful' rather than 'dull' might be seen as making the best of a bad job, but the fact is that in dark shade we have to be grateful to find anything that will grow. The hart's tongue fern mentioned above and ivies are among the limited range worth trying. In less deep shade it is possible to provide some 'light' by growing white or pale-coloured flowers, and especially by planting variegated varieties. In deeper shade, however, attractively flowering plants rarely flourish, and variegated plants react to the low light levels by turning green!

The shade cast by buildings at least does not normally restrict light coming from directly above, although poor soil quality and drought along walls can further reduce the ability of plants to grow. In the worst instances, areas with impoverished, dry soil in light shade have to be treated as 'dry' shade, where only the most tolerant species will be able to flourish.

It is futile to deny that dry shade is difficult for the gardener. Shade can be dry because of proximity to a building, or because thirsty trees suck moisture out of the ground. The selection of plants is definitely wider, and a little more attractive, than for deep shade, although it is still limited. Various grass-like, and gratifyingly evergreen, plants, such as the rather majestic pendulous sedge (*Carex pendula*) and the wood rushes (*Luzula* spp.), will grow reasonably well, along with some ferns and a few flowering plants. Of the ferns, soft shield fern (*Polystichium*

setiferum) is a godsend, the attractive fronds intricately divided like the finest lace, and there are a number of different varieties available. Of flowering plants *Geranium himalayense* (syn. *G. grandiflorum*), which is summer flowering and mauve-blue, and *G. macrorrhizum*, which is early summer flowering and pink, are the among the most rewarding and reliable. For spring, the early-flowering *Euphorbia amygdaloides* var. *robbiae* is worth remembering, with its yellow-green flowers and a somewhat invasive habit. At least in difficult shade the latter quality can become something of a virtue.

Whereas 'easy' shade allows the gardener to build an attractive mosaic of low-growing, shade-loving plants, where spring flowers bloom among a wide variety of leaf shapes and textures, the problems of deep or dry shade allow no such recreation of woodland reverie. The best way to create artistic impact is to block plant, growing several individuals of one variety together to develop a patchwork effect.

Bamboo is an elegant space filler for many shady sites. Here it is contrasted effectively with a ground cover of ivy.

Block planting with shade-tolerant plants

Dry and other difficult shade is most effectively planted in single-species blocks using ground-cover plants. Here, on the left an ivy (*Hedera helix*) is used as ground cover, along with the grassy snowy woodrush (*Luzula nivea*) in the centre. On the right-hand side, *Geranium macrorrhizum* receives the most light. To provide some variation in the ground cover, taller, more architectural foliage plants can be used at intervals – here pendulous sedge (*Carex pendula*).

Gradations in Shade

Next time you go for a woodland walk, take a look at how the wildflowers grow. In the deepest shade there may be little or nothing (certainly nothing you'd want to pay money for at a nursery). Where there is more light there is a lot more vegetation, but it tends to be restricted to a small number of species. Where there is more light still, perhaps some sunlight for part of the day, in a woodland glade or along a path, there is a sudden increase in the number of species and in the luxuriance of the vegetation. At the woodland edge there is sometimes a thicket of shrubs and climbers alternating with light grass and a rich variety of perennial wildflowers.

In gardens where there is plenty of space this woodland edge thicket can be imitated with attractive shrubs that are tolerant of light shade, planted at the edge of tree canopies acting as a screen. It is important that this is done only with mature trees, otherwise the shrubs will end up getting shaded out as the trees grow.

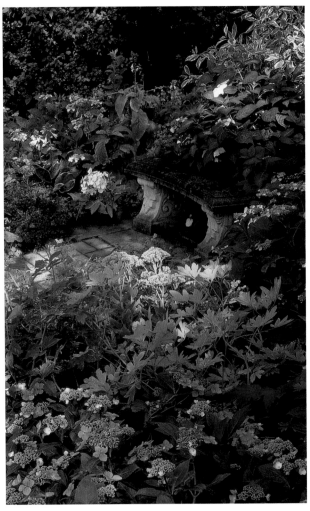

Few shrubs do well in shade; hydrangeas (this is 'Blue Wave') often will, and they flower after the majority of spring and early-summer shade-loving perennials have finished.

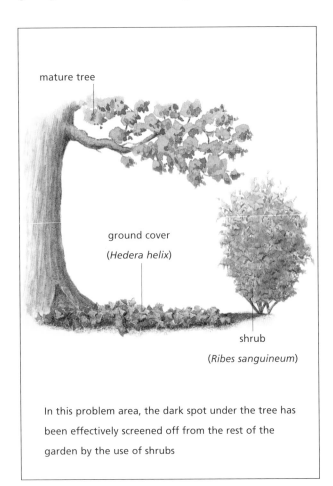

mature tree

ground cover
(*Hedera helix*)

shrub
(*Ribes sanguineum*)

In this problem area, the dark spot under the tree has been effectively screened off from the rest of the garden by the use of shrubs

Many of the characteristic wildflowers of the woodland edge are favourite garden plants – aquilegias, foxgloves and the hardy geraniums (cranesbills), for instance. These are often taller, faster growing and more brightly coloured than plants for full shade. They also tend to flower a little later, in late spring to early summer. In the garden, it is well worth remembering the natural gradation in plant species variety from light to deep shade. Lovers of full shade can be planted under trees, with the half-shade plants at the outer edges of the tree canopy. Given the taller habit and later flowering of many of the latter, they will grow up and to an extent hide the lower growing full-shade plants as the summer progresses.

Three zones of shade under a deciduous tree

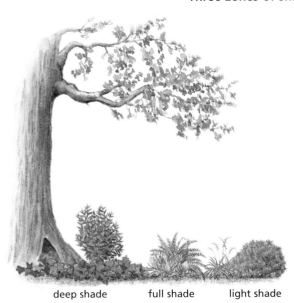

deep shade   full shade   light shade

Spring

deep shade   full shade   light shade

Early to midsummer

In the deep shade at the far left only an ivy (*Hedera* spp.) and butcher's broom (*Ruscus aculeatus*) grow. In spring the full- and light-shade zones are full of low-growing flowers, such as crocus and scilla, along with some evergreen ferns. In summer this area is largely green with deciduous ferns, although there are some early-summer flowers, such as woodruff (*Galium odoratum*). The area of light shade really comes into its own in early midsummer, with a mixture of low perennials, such as *Geranium endressii*, and taller perennials, such as *Campanula latifolia* and foxgloves (*Digitalis purpurea*).

Plant Directory

Luxuriant Growers for Moist Shade

Moist shade offers an opportunity to grow a wide variety of interesting, often spectacular, plants, the majority of which are early to midsummer flowering or are notable for their foliage. It is also ideal for many ferns.

Astilbe

- Herbaceous perennial
- 60–120 x 60–90cm (2–4 x 2–3ft)
- Plumes of pink, red or white flowers are borne in early summer over lush clumps of divided foliage. Astilbes look very good with ferns and hostas.
- Plant in sun or light shade; they need damp ground to do well.

Ligularia
(leopard plant)

- Herbaceous perennial
- 90–180 x 60cm (3–6 x 2ft)
- A group of luxuriant midsummer-flowering yellow daisies. *L. dentata* 'Desdemona' has orange-yellow flowers and dark bronzy, heart-shaped leaves. *L.* 'The Rocket' has spires of yellow flowers above triangular foliage.
- Plant in sun or light shade and in damp, fertile soil. Ligularias are prone to slug damage.

Matteucia struthiopteris
(ostrich fern, shuttlecock fern)

- Herbaceous fern
- 60 x 60cm (24 x 24in)
- The extremely elegant, light green fronds are held in a 'vase' shape, and the fern needs space to be seen at its best. Combine it with lower growing plants.
- Plant in damp soil and light shade.

Osmunda regalis
(royal fern)

- Herbaceous fern
- 1.2 x 0.9m (4 x 3ft)
- This is one of the most majestic of hardy plants. The fronds are large and relatively undivided and there are brown fertile fronds in the centre of the plant. It does best by water or among lower growing vegetation.
- Plant in light shade or in sun; damp, acid soil is essential.

Primula – candelabra types

- Herbaceous perennials
- 60–90 x 40cm (24–36 x 16in)
- So-called because of the whorls of flower surrounding the tall stem, candelabra primulas flower in early to midsummer, and they can naturalize in damp places. *P. japonica* is bright pink; *P. pulverulenta* is paler; *P. helodoxa* is yellow; and there are many unnamed hybrids. They look good with hostas and rodgersias.
- Plant in damp soil in sun or light shade.

Further suggestions
Aruncus spp.; *Astilboides tabularis*; *Clethra arborea* (lily-of-the-valley tree); *Darmera peltata* (syn. *Peltiphyllum peltatum*; umbrella plant); *Geranium* spp.; *Hosta* spp.; *Kalmia latifolia* (calico bush); *Leucojum* spp. (snowflake), *Phlox paniculata*; *Physostegia virginiana*; *Polygonum* spp.; *Prunus laurocerasus* (cherry laurel); *Rodgersia* spp.; most ferns and indeed most shade-lovers if the ground is not actually waterlogged

Dry-shade Tolerators
The following are likely to be the most attractive plants for this difficult habitat, providing a long season of foliage interest and some spring to early-summer colour. It is worth experimenting: if you already have some shade-tolerant plants, try planting out some divisions in the dry spots. You might make some interesting discoveries.

Euphorbia amygdaloides var. *robbiae*
- Strongly spreading evergreen herbaceous perennial
- 60 x 60cm (24 x 24in)
- Dark leaves and yellow-green flowers in early spring in difficult shade are good reasons to forgive this euphorbia its aggressively running root system. Plant in any reasonable soil.

Euphorbia characias subsp. *wulfenii*
- Evergreen perennial
- 1 x 1m (3 x 3ft)
- Grey foliage and rather intriguing pale green flowers are borne in early spring, unfurling over a period of weeks. A very robust and adaptable plant, it thrives alongside other grey-leaved plants in sun and lower ground cover in shade.
- Plant in any reasonable soil.

Geranium macrorrhizum
- Spreading, clump-forming herbaceous perennial
- 30 x 60cm (12 x 24in)
- Bright pink, or white or pale pink, depending on variety, this geranium is remarkably resilient, flowering in early summer. Its strongly aromatic leaves are reputed to keep cats away. Easily divided to propagate for ground cover.
- Plant in sun or light shade and in any reasonable soil.

Luzula
(woodrush)

- Slowly spreading, evergreen, grass-like plant
- 30 x 30cm (12 x 12in)
- A quietly attractive plant that looks good all year round. Common woodruff (*L. sylvatica*) has broad leaves; snowy woodrush (*L. nivea*) has finer leaves and short-lived cream flowers in early summer. Divide or sow seed to propogate for ground cover.
- Plant in shade and in any reasonable soil.

Polystichum setiferum
(soft shield fern)

- Evergreen fern
- 90 x 90cm (36 x 36in)
- Finely divided fronds make this a very fetching plant for dry shade or, if the soil is moister, for sun. There are various forms with even more intensely divided leaves and these are usually more compact in habit.
- Plant in any reasonable soil.

Further suggestions

Buxus sempervirens (box); *Cyclamen hederifolium*; *Ilex aquifolium* (common holly); *Iris foetidissima* (gladwin, stinking iris); *Lamium galeobdolon* (deadnettle); *Symphytum* spp. (comfrey); *Tellima grandiflora* (fringecups); *Vinca* spp. (periwinkle)

Deep-shade Plants

Deep shade is another very difficult environment. Most of the following are worthy, if not breathtaking, plants, and all are dark evergreens with architectural rather than floral interest. They are, however, an awful lot better than nothing at all.

Asplenium scolopendrium
(syn. *Phyllitis scolopendrium*; hart's tongue fern)

- Evergreen fern
- 30 x 40cm (12 x 16in)
- The fact that this is the last plant to be seen down a well recommends this fern, with its distinctive strap-shaped fronds, for dark, but not too dry, places. There are numerous forms with crinkly or otherwise ornamented foliage.
- This fern tolerates light shade but not direct sun.

Danae racemosa (Alexandrian laurel)
and ***Ruscus aculeatus*** (butcher's broom)

- Slowly spreading evergreen perennials
- 1m (3ft) x ultimately 1m (3ft)
- These are two very similar plants for deep shade, with dark stems and leaves and an arching habit of growth. Red berries are occasionally produced.
- Plant in deep to light shade and in any reasonable soil.

Hedera helix
(ivy)

- Evergreen climber
- Here, suggested as a trailer, at 1m (3ft) planting distances
- The number-one cheap and easy way to fill deep shade is with a common and self-propagating plant. Only deep green varieties will grow here, however; the variegated ones go green in dark shade.

Anemone blanda

Early-season Colour

This is definitely the time of year for shade. The following tend to be among the earliest flowers in the garden. With the exceptions of *Lamium maculatum* (a perennial), they are all bulbs or tubers and are good for growing around the base of trees, even if there is light grass there. Over time, they will naturalize – that is, begin to spread on their own. They can look effective mixed together.

Anemone blanda

- Slowly spreading tuberous perennial
- 10 x 10cm (4 x 4in)
- Blue, pink or white flowers, almost daisy-like in appearance, for shade or in light grass at the foot of trees, where they will naturalize, spreading by seed. Flowers appear in early spring.
- Plant in any reasonable soil.

Cyclamen coum

- Tuberous perennial
- 7 x 10cm (3 x 4in)
- The magenta, or in some varieties, paler pink or white, flowers look wonderful with snowdrops underneath trees and in other shaded places in mid- to late winter. They will self-seed given time.
- Good drainage is essential.

Eranthis hyemalis

(syn. *Aconitum hyemalis*; winter aconite)

- Tuberous perennial
- 7 x 10cm (3 x 4in)
- Yellow flowers appear in shade or in the grass underneath trees in late winter, and will form extensive patches by seeding if allowed to – that is, don't mow the grass until the leaves have started to yellow. Like snowdrops, they are best transplanted in leaf.

Galanthus nivalis

(snowdrop)

- Bulb
- 10 x 8cm (4 x 3½in)
- Pure white flowers in late winter mark the onset of spring. Snowdrops do well at the foot of trees and will form substantial clumps with time. These can be spread by transplanting 'in the green' – that is, during or after flowering time.
- Plant in any reasonable soil.

Lamium maculatum

(deadnettle)

- Spreading semi-evergreen perennial
- 10 x 40cm (4 x 16in)
- White-blotched leaves usually appear early, making good ground cover with flowers to follow later in spring. *L. m.* 'Beacon Silver' has white-silver foliage; *L. m.* 'White Nancy' has white flowers.
- Plant in light to full shade and in moist but well-drained soil.

Further suggestions

Bergenia spp. (elephant's ear); *Convallaria* spp. (lily-of-the-valley); *Corydalis* spp.; *Epimedium* spp.; *Helleborus* spp. (hellebores); *Pulmonaria* spp. (lungwort)

Lamium maculatum

Late-season Colour

Given that most shade-tolerant plants flower early, the rest of the year can be rather dependent on the foliage. These plants are all useful for an end-of-season burst of colour, even though most of them are white. They are all long-lived plants that do best if left alone to look after themselves.

Anemone x hybrida

(syn. *A. japonica*)

- Slowly spreading, clump-forming perennial
- 1.5 x 0.6m (5 x 2ft)
- A number of anemones flower from midsummer to early autumn, with the pure white of *A. x h.* 'Honorine Jobert' being superlative. There are various pink hybrids as well, including some rather hard, deep shades, and doubles, too. They like being left undisturbed.
- Plant in light shade or sun, in moist, fertile but well-drained soil.

Aster divaricatus and A. macrophyllus

- Spreading herbaceous perennials
- 60 x 60cm (24 x 24in)
- White daisy flowers brighten up shady places in late summer to early autumn. *A. macrophyllus* has pale blue flowers.
- Plant in light to full shade and in any reasonable soil. Both species are seemingly tolerant of some dry shade.

Cimicifuga

(bugbane)

- Erect-growing herbaceous perennials
- 90–120 x 60cm (3–4 x 2ft)
- Tall spires of tightly packed, little cream flowers are the mark of

the summer- to early autumn-flowering bugbanes. Their divided foliage is attractive too, especially in the purple-tinged *C. simplex* var. *simplex* Atropurpurea Group. *C. simplex* is the latest to flower.

- They need cool conditions in shade in moist, well-drained soil.

Eupatorium aromaticum and *E. rugosum* (mist flower)

- Slowly spreading, erect-growing herbaceous perennial
- 70 x 30cm (28 x 12in)
- White fluffy flowerheads illuminate shady corners from late summer to early autumn.
- Plant in shade or sun, if not too dry, and any reasonable soil.

Liriope muscari (lilyturf)

- Slowly spreading, clump-forming evergreen perennial
- 30 x 40cm (12 x 6in)
- Narrow, somewhat grass-like leaves send up spikes of densely packed violet flowers in autumn.
- Plant in light shade or sun and in any reasonable soil.

Further suggestions
Actaea spp.
(baneberry)

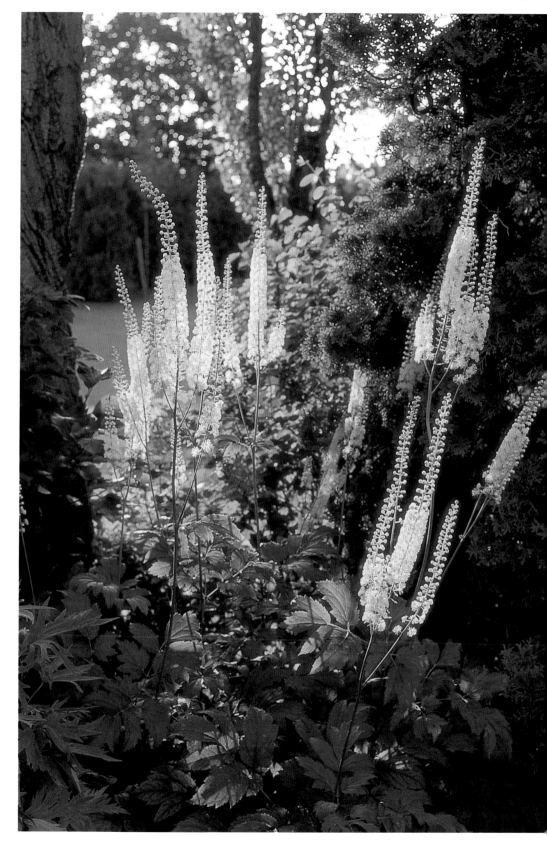

Cimicifuga racemosa

'Problem'.
sites

I have put the word 'problem' in inverted commas because I am rather sceptical about describing as 'problems' gardens that have a particular feature such as waterlogged soil, frequent droughts, exposure to the wind, a position on the coast, acid or alkaline soils and so on. They are only necessarily problem gardens if you want to grow nothing more than the most conventional range of garden plants. As we saw in the section on shade, what may at first seem undesirable can, in fact, allow us to grow a wide variety of very attractive plants, some of which might not thrive in a 'normal' sunny garden.

The fact is that among the vast number of plants now available it is always possible to find a decent number of attractive plants to transform what may at first seem like inhospitable conditions. Sometimes they are really quite spectacular. Reference books that give plenty of information about the habitat preferences of plants are most useful in tracking down suitable species, as are those books on the particular environment concerned. It is also important that you develop a feel for the habitat your garden presents. The diagrams in this chapter are intended to help you focus on the 'plant forms' that tend to dominate particular environments naturally. Focusing on these will make easier the task of selecting plants that are naturally adapted to cope with difficult conditions.

Waterlogged Soil

Ground that experiences periodic flooding can reduce the number of plants that will thrive, but it does mean that

Above: Wet soil is a fantastic opportunity to grow so many colourful flowers and plants with lush foliage, all of which establish remarkably rapidly.

water is never far below the surface, no matter how dry it looks in summer. Moisture-loving plants grow rapidly and look lush and extravagant; most are summer-flowering perennials. Such a site should be an inspiration to grow lots of big perennials and reedy grasses.

The year can start off with kingcups (*Caltha* spp.), move on later in spring with blue camassias and a selection of blue and yellow irises and pink and red astilbes, before coming to the high point of the wetland year: midsummer. Large yellow ligularias, cream and white meadowsweet (*Filipendula* spp.), pinky rodgersias and the eupatoriums all flower now. A group of blue and purple asters and pure white *Leucanthemella serotina* (syn. *Chrysanthemum serotinum*, *C. uliginosum*) can finish up the year. Grasses, such as varieties of *Miscanthus* and *Molinia*, can be the source of much winter pleasure.

PLANTING SUGGESTIONS
Small trees and shrubs

Amelanchier spp. (serviceberry); *Cornus alba* (red-barked dogwood), *C. stolonifera* (red osier dogwood); *Crataegus laevigata* (syn. *C. oxyacantha*; hawthorn, may); *Liquidamber styraciflua*

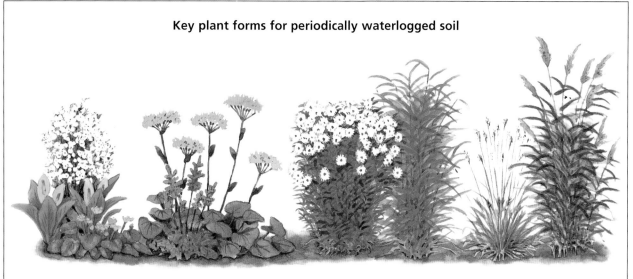

Key plant forms for periodically waterlogged soil

Spring: relatively few early perennials, such as marsh marigold (*Caltha palustris*) and yellow skunk cabbage (*Lysichiton americanus*); flowering shrubs, such as *Amelanchier lamarckii*

Summer: large perennials, such as *Astilbe* hybrids and *Ligularia* species

Autumn: large perennials, such as *Leucanthemella serotina*, and grasses, such as *Miscanthus sinensis*

Winter: seedheads of perennials and grasses

(sweet gum); *Metasequoia glyptostroboides* (dawn redwood); *Physocarpus opulifolius* (ninebark); *Salix* spp. (willow); *Sambucus* spp. (elder); *Sorbus aucuparia* (mountain ash, rowan); *Spiraea* x *vanhouttei* (bridal wreath); bamboos (if not actually waterlogged); most climbers will flourish if the ground is not waterlogged for long periods

Perennials and bulbs

Aster novi-belgii; *Astilbe* spp.; *Caltha* spp.; *Camassia* spp.; *Eupatorium* spp.; *Euphorbia palustris*; *Filipendula* spp. (meadowsweet); *Geranium* spp.; *Gunnera* spp.; *Hosta* spp.; *Iris ensata* (syn. *I. kaempferi*; Japanese flag), *I. pseudacorus* (yellow flag), *I. sibirica* (Siberian flag), *I. versicolor* (blue flag, wild iris);

Leucanthemella serotina (syn. *Chrysanthemum serotinum*, *C. uliginosum*); *Leucojum* spp. (snowflake); *Ligularia* spp.; *Lobelia* spp.; *Lysichiton* spp. (skunk cabbage, bog arum); *Lysimachia* spp. (loosestrife); *Lythrum* spp. (purple loosestrife); *Miscanthus* spp.; *Molinia* spp.; *Persicaria* spp. (knotweed); *Rheum* spp. (ornamental rhubarb); *Rodgersia* spp.; *Thalictrum* spp. (meadow rue); *Trollius* spp. (globeflower); *Veronica* spp.; most ferns if the ground is not actually waterlogged

Dry Gardens and Drought

Thin, stony and light, sandy soils dry out rapidly, even more so if they face the sun on a slope. The kind of plants that survive where others fail tend to be very distinctive

– mostly low, evergreen shrubs, often with grey foliage; bulbs; small, often mat-forming perennials; and annuals. Holidays in areas with Mediterranean climates or other temperate but drought-prone areas will give you a feel of the kind of plants that survive.

Late winter and spring can be colourful indeed, as there is a rush to flower and seed before the sun gets too hot and the soil too dry. Bulbs, such as wild tulips and grape hyacinths (*Muscari* spp.), provide intense colours. Later, bearded irises, red valerian (*Centranthus ruber*), rock roses (*Cistus* spp., *Helianthemum* spp.) in a wide variety of colours and dwarf pinks (*Dianthus* spp.) are just a few of the many colourful plants that will flower in early summer. Late summer sees something of a reduction in flowers, although there will still be catmint (*Nepeta* spp.) and lavenders (*Lavandula* spp.). Since many of the most colourful annuals, such as poppies, come from semi-desert environments, these can be used for mid- to late summer colour. Grasses such as golden oats (*Stipa gigantea*) can look wonderful in the autumn, and the greys and silvers of the dwarf shrubs provide plenty of winter interest.

PLANTING SUGGESTIONS

Small trees and shrubs

Abelia spp.; *Artemisia* spp. (wormwood); *Berberis* spp.; *Betula* spp. (birch); *Buddleja* spp. (buddleia); *Cistus* spp. (rock rose); *Cotoneaster* spp.; *Cytisus* spp. (broom); *Elaeagnus* spp.; *Fremontodendron californicum*; *Genista* spp. (broom); *Hypericum* spp.; *Ilex* spp. (holly); *Lavandula* spp. (lavender); *Olearia* spp. (daisy bush); *Phlomis* spp.; *Potentilla* spp.; *Rhus* spp. (sumac); *Ribes* spp. (ornamental currant); *Santolina* spp.; *Tamarix* spp. (tamarisk); *Teucrium* spp.; *Yucca* spp.

Perennials and bulbs

Achillea spp. (milfoil, yarrow); *Allium* spp. (onion); *Anaphalis* spp. (pearl everlasting); *Aster amellus*; *Centranthus* spp.; *Colchicum* spp. (autumn crocus); *Dianthus* spp. (pinks); *Elymus* spp.; *Eremurus* spp. (foxtail lily); *Eryngium* spp. (sea holly); *Festuca* spp. (fescue); *Iris germanica* (common German flag) and similar with broad, grey foliage and 'bearded' flowers; *Muscari* spp. (grape hyacinth); *Nepeta* spp. (catmint); *Origanum* spp. (marjoram, dittany); *Papaver* spp. (poppy); *Pennisetum* spp.; *Perovskia* spp.; *Rosmarinus* spp. (rosemary); *Salvia* spp. (sage); *Stipa* spp.; *Tulipa* spp. (tulip); *Verbascum* spp. (mullein)

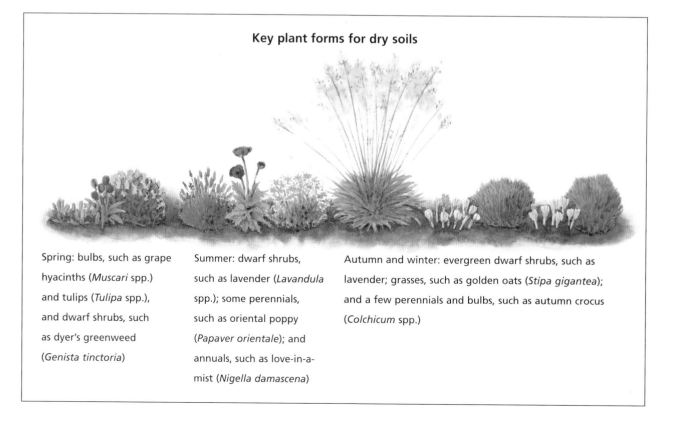

Key plant forms for dry soils

Spring: bulbs, such as grape hyacinths (*Muscari* spp.) and tulips (*Tulipa* spp.), and dwarf shrubs, such as dyer's greenweed (*Genista tinctoria*)

Summer: dwarf shrubs, such as lavender (*Lavandula* spp.); some perennials, such as oriental poppy (*Papaver orientale*); and annuals, such as love-in-a-mist (*Nigella damascena*)

Autumn and winter: evergreen dwarf shrubs, such as lavender; grasses, such as golden oats (*Stipa gigantea*); and a few perennials and bulbs, such as autumn crocus (*Colchicum* spp.)

The characteristic plants of dry soils tend to flower spectacularly. Here *Gladiolus byzantinus* and a verbascum bring colour to a drought-prone border.

Cold and Exposure

'Cold' in a garden can mean a number of things. It can be a place that is sheltered from the wind but, because of the lie of the land, experiences regular and severe frosts. Alternatively, it could be a site that is exposed to cold and penetrating winds but has few hard frosts. In either case, plant selection has to be done carefully, because those not up to the hard conditions may not last long.

Many of the perennials commonly grown in gardens come from regions, such as North America, that have bitterly cold winters, making them first-rate plants for cold areas. A wide variety of bulbs is very hardy too, although those from Central Asia or the Mediterranean may not tolerate a combination of cold and damp in the soil. It stands to reason that plants that are tucked out of harm's way underground are going to be at less risk of succumbing to harsh weather than those woody plants that are more exposed to the elements. Late spring frosts or cold winds can, however, damage their tender new growth.

The choice of trees and shrubs needs to be made particularly carefully in cold areas. Those regions that have continental climates may see many shrubs widely regarded as hardy, including several roses, cut to the ground by some winters, making them all but herbaceous plants. There are, however, plenty of very hardy small trees from which to choose – birches (*Betula* spp.), rowans (*Sorbus* spp.), the serviceberry (*Amelanchier* spp.) and flowering cherries and apples (*Prunus* and *Malus* spp.).

PLANTING SUGGESTIONS

Small trees and shrubs

Amelanchier spp. (serviceberry); *Betula* spp. (birch), *Calluna vulgaris* (heather); *Cornus alba* (red-barked dogwood), *C. stolonifera* (red osier dogwood); *Crataegus* spp. (hawthorn); *Cotinus coggygria* (syn. *Rhus cotinus*; smoke tree); *Euonymus fortunei*; *Kalmia latifolia* (calico bush); *Laburnum* spp.; *Malus* spp. (apple); *Philadelphus* spp. (mock orange); *Prunus* spp. (cherry); *Salix* spp. (willow); *Sorbus* spp. (rowan); *Spiraea* spp.; *Tamarix* spp. (tamarisk)

Key plant forms for cold and exposed areas

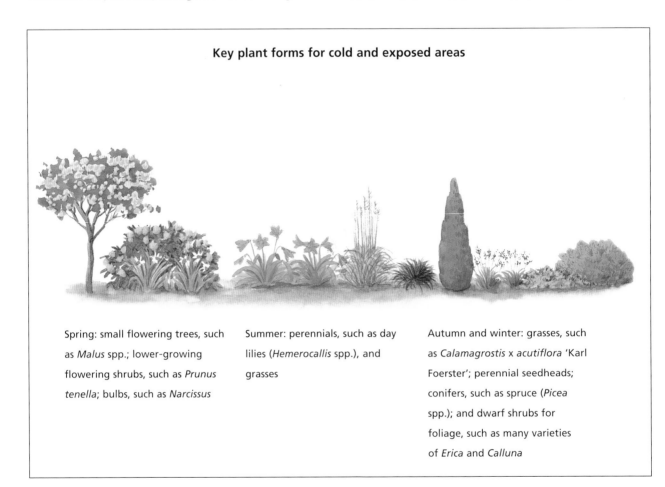

Spring: small flowering trees, such as *Malus* spp.; lower-growing flowering shrubs, such as *Prunus tenella*; bulbs, such as *Narcissus*

Summer: perennials, such as day lilies (*Hemerocallis* spp.), and grasses

Autumn and winter: grasses, such as *Calamagrostis* x *acutiflora* 'Karl Foerster'; perennial seedheads; conifers, such as spruce (*Picea* spp.); and dwarf shrubs for foliage, such as many varieties of *Erica* and *Calluna*

Perennials, grasses and bulbs

Nearly all perennials, grasses and bulbs commonly available, the height of the plant being the limiting factor in windy areas; obviously the shorter the plant the more wind resistant it will be. Grasses, however tall, are wind resistant, simply bending over

Coastal Gardens

The coast is always a special place, often with wonderful views and a special quality of light. Yet it can be difficult for plants: cold or very strong winds, salt spray and occasional drought because soils are often poor. Some coastal areas actually have very mild climates, with strong but not cold winds, which allow species to be grown that would not survive only a short way inland.

Many plants with grey or silver leaves survive dehydration and will, therefore, do well at the coast, as will most that have fleshy or waxy leaves. Choosing evergreens needs to be done on the basis of local experience, because the foliage is particularly vulnerable to winter gales. As with cold areas, perennials (lower growing ones rather than taller) and bulbs are good coastal plants, emerging as they do after the worst of the winter weather has subsided. Many of the low-growing shrubs from Mediterranean or semi-desert climates discussed under Dry

Allium giganteum presides over a selection of the kind of plants that flourish in windswept coastal conditions: grasses and grey-leaved species from Mediterranean climates.

Gardens and Drought (see pages 105–7) will be successful. Shrubs and trees need to be chosen on the basis of local knowledge and recommendation. Remembering what has been said about resistant kinds of foliage above, one soon gets a feel for what will survive.

Ornamental grasses are perhaps the single most valuable group of plants for coastal gardens. The taller ones can be relied on for structure in the garden, and the dwarfer ones for foliage colour and for filling gaps between shrubs. Grasses seem singularly appropriate to coasts, their beauty often matching that of the environment.

PLANTING SUGGESTIONS

Small trees and shrubs

Arbutus spp. (strawberry tree); *Choisya ternata* (Mexican orange blossom); *Cordyline australis* (New Zealand cabbage palm); *Cotoneaster* spp.; *Crataegus* spp. (hawthorn); *Cytisus* spp. (broom); *Elaeagnus* spp.; *Escallonia* spp.; *Euonymus fortunei*; *E. japonicus* (Japanese spindle); *Fuchsia* spp., *Genista* spp. (broom); *Griselinia littoralis* (broadleaf); *Hebe* spp. (shrubby veronica); *Helianthemum* spp. (rock rose); *Olearia* spp. (daisy bush); *Phlomis* spp.; *Phormium* spp. (New Zealand flax); *Pittosporum* spp.; *Salix* spp. (willow); *Santolina* spp.; *Senecio* spp.; *Sorbus* spp. (rowan); *Tamarix* spp. (tamarisk); *Viburnum* spp.; *Yucca* spp.

Perennials, grasses and bulbs

Shorter perennials, most bulbs and all grasses, even taller ones

Acid Soils

Acid soils tend to be infertile, lacking sufficient quantities of a number of the nutrients needed by many plants to grow. In nature acid soils are covered in vegetation composed of plants adapted to grow in such conditions, and fortunately for us several of these plants are truly spectacular species, to the point where many gardeners are delighted to discover that they have acid soil. There is little cause for despair here, although if you have set your heart on growing roses, you might have to reconsider your plans.

Spring is an extremely rewarding time in gardens on acid soils: rhododendrons, azaleas, camellias and a wide variety of woodland plants can provide non-stop colour right through from the end of winter until midsummer.

From then there is a more limited number of shrubs that will give colour in the garden. Herbaceous perennials can be used in borders for late-season interest, although most do not do as well as they would on more fertile soils. Heathers can be used to fill the gap instead,

Right: Acid soils can be made very colourful in spring, with many shrubs, such as rhododendrons, flourishing where others do not. Where soils do not dry out, Japanese maples will thrive as well.

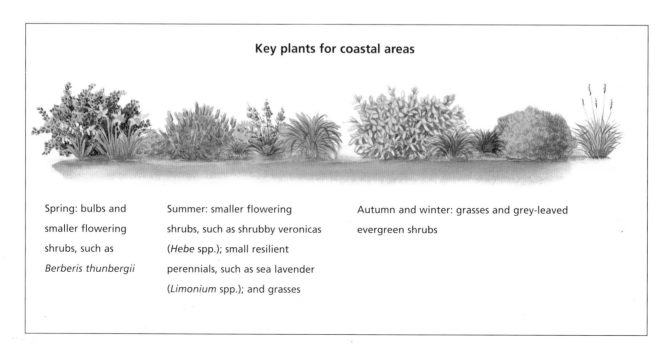

Key plants for coastal areas

Spring: bulbs and smaller flowering shrubs, such as *Berberis thunbergii*

Summer: smaller flowering shrubs, such as shrubby veronicas (*Hebe* spp.); small resilient perennials, such as sea lavender (*Limonium* spp.); and grasses

Autumn and winter: grasses and grey-leaved evergreen shrubs

Key plants for acid soil

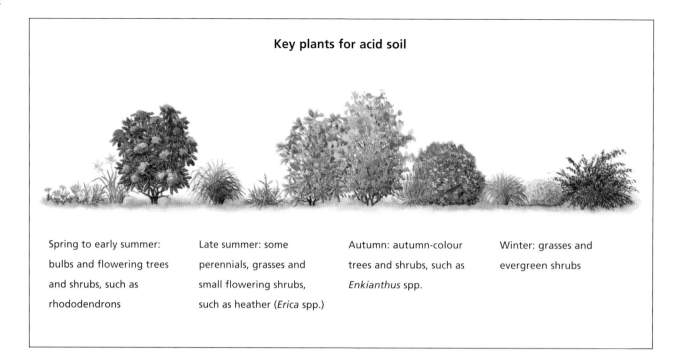

Spring to early summer: bulbs and flowering trees and shrubs, such as rhododendrons

Late summer: some perennials, grasses and small flowering shrubs, such as heather (*Erica* spp.)

Autumn: autumn-colour trees and shrubs, such as *Enkianthus* spp.

Winter: grasses and evergreen shrubs

the widest selection of varieties coming into flower when the larger spring and early-summer shrubs are finishing. Many heathers will continue to flower into the winter, and some develop bronze or yellow foliage during cold weather.

The autumn colour of trees, such as many American oaks (*Quercus coccinea*, for example) and Japanese maples (*Acer palmatum*), usually develops best on acid soils, something those on 'better' soils may well envy. Grasses and sedges look at their best now too, most continuing to give interest through the winter.

PLANTING SUGGESTIONS

Small trees and shrubs

Acer palmatum (Japanese maple); *Betula* spp. (birch); *Calluna vulgaris* (heather); *Camellia* spp; *Cistus* spp. (rock rose); *Clethra* spp.; *Cornus* spp.; *Cotoneaster* spp.; *Cytisus* spp. (broom); *Enkianthus* spp.; *Erica* spp. (heather); *Genista* spp. (broom); *Kalmia* spp.; *Magnolia* spp.; *Pernettya* spp.; *Photinia* spp.; *Pieris* spp.; *Rhododendron* spp.; *Rosa pimpinellifolia* (syn. *R. spinosissima*; burnet rose), *R. rugosa*; *Skimmia* spp.; *Stewartia* spp.; *Vaccinium* spp.

Perennials, bulbs and climbers

Practically all will grow satisfactorily if soil conditions are reasonably fertile

Alkaline Soils

Many very alkaline soils – that is, soils containing a lot of lime – are thin, overlaying limestone or chalk. They tend to be on the poor side and often become dry in summer droughts. Larger perennials and many shrubs, including roses, do not thrive in such conditions. What succeed very well, however, are many of the plants that do well on dry soils generally, including many of the low-growing, mat-forming plants that are sold as rockery plants but often become too vigorous for the rock garden – including species of *Dianthus*, *Campanula* (harebells and the related bellflowers), yellow hypericums and cloudy white gypsophilas. Many wildflowers thrive, too, making the creation of a wildflower meadow a possibility. The soil is too dry and poor for strong grass growth, which allows the more stress-tolerant wildflowers a chance to succeed.

Late winter and spring are the best times on thin alkaline soils. The lime-tolerant winter heather (*Erica carnea*) can start the year off, followed by the various kinds of low-growing small perennials just discussed. Dwarf shrubs of the lavender and cistus (rock rose) type are the most reliable sources of summer colour, along with those shrubs that do succeed on these soils, such as brooms (*Cytisus* and *Genista* spp.), pink and white spiraeas and shrubby veronicas (*Hebe* spp.). Hebes are useful for the many kinds that have late-summer or even autumn flowers. Autumn and early-winter interest must depend on a few shrubs such as these and on grasses, most of which flourish, especially the lower growing ones.

PLANTING SUGGESTIONS

Small trees and shrubs

Berberis spp.; *Caryopteris* spp.; *Ceanothus* spp.; *Cercis* spp. (Judas tree); *Cistus* spp. (rock rose); *Coronilla* spp.; *Cotoneaster* spp.; *Crataegus laevigata* (syn. *C. oxyacantha*; hawthorn, may); *Daphne* mezereum (mezereon), *D. odora*; *Deutzia* spp.; *Forsythia* spp.; *Fremontodendron californicum*; *Genista* spp. (broom); *Hebe* spp. (shrubby veronica); *Laburnum* spp.; *Liquidamber styraciflua* (sweet gum); *Malus* spp. (apple); *Olearia* spp. (daisy bush); *Photinia* spp.; *Potentilla* spp.; *Rosa* spp. (rose); *Rosmarinus* spp. (rosemary); *Sambucus* spp. (elder); *Senecio* spp.; *Sorbus* spp. (rowan); *Syringa* spp. (lilac); *Yucca* spp.

Perennials and bulbs

Nearly all will grow, drought and fertility being the limiting factors. As a very general rule, the smaller the species the better it will cope with particularly dry and/or infertile alkaline soils

---

Key plants for alkaline soil

Spring: bulbs, shrubs and low-growing, rockery-type plants, such as pinks (*Dianthus* spp.)

Summer: low-growing, rockery-type and wildflowers, such as *Campanula* spp., grasses and lower growing shrubs

Autumn and winter: grasses and lower growing evergreen shrubs

Containers

The great advantage of growing plants in containers is that they are moveable, giving the gardener the opportunity instantly to transform any part of the garden they choose to. A moveable garden is a flexible one. Some containers, of course, are not easily moved or are not intended to be, either because, like classical urns, they are used as focal points and are meant to stay where they are put or simply because they are too heavy. Containers are especially useful in situations where there is no soil in which to grow plants – courtyards, roof gardens, balconies and terraces, for example. They may, indeed, be the only spaces some people have in which to garden. More than anything else, the use of plants in pots and tubs can transform hard concrete-dominated spaces.

A mixture of permanent and seasonal planting may be the best use of containers in such a space. Permanent plantings provide continuity, especially if they are chosen for their evergreen foliage or structure. Yet seasonal plants enable you to use species that provide concentrated colour and interest, and you can discard them as soon as they begin to tire. In this way, a garden in a limited space will have only plants that are at their best all the time.

Pelargoniums, petunias and other bedding plants have long been favourites for the summer, and have now been joined by a wide range of other half-hardy plants. Yet there is no reason why plantings cannot be created for other seasons, especially in permanently placed containers, which look bare if there is nothing in them. Bulbs are the obvious choice in spring, along with small cold-weather

Above: Nothing conjures up hot sunny thoughts like containers full of colourful exotic-looking plants; this is scarlet *Cyrtanthus elatus* with succulents.

bedding plants, such as pansies and polyanthus. Winter plantings can be made with very early-flowering heathers and small, easy-to-establish perennials, such as varieties of deadnettle (*Lamium* spp.) and bugle (*Ajuga* spp.), many of which have coloured foliage as well as bright flowers.

Containers in the Garden

Standing containers around the garden is much less common than using them on hard surfaces. Some might think it pointless: why bother humping a heavy pot around when there is perfectly good soil underneath? But what it gives is flexibility and the opportunity to make instant and temporary transformations to selected parts of the garden.

Maybe part of the garden is looking a bit dull – then move in a pot full of cheerfully flowering plants, which will bring life to the area for a few weeks. Pots of flowering plants can even be moved around into shady areas on a rota basis – a week or two in a gloomy spot, followed by a few weeks back in the sun to recuperate. Plants

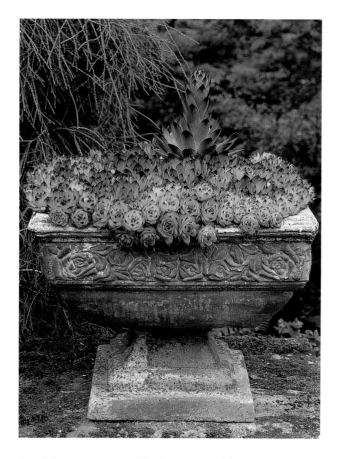

Simplicity is often more effective than anything; a semper-vivum is a drought-tolerant option for a shallow container.

points or provide a 'change of pace' in a garden with plenty of planting but few hard edges. The better the container, the more important is the choice of plant to live in it. Plants should not overwhelm the container or vice versa, but each be in proportion to the other. Ideally, their colours should relate to each other, too, perhaps with some of the plants picking out the colour of the container.

Mobile plants can also be used to great effect if their containers are hidden, the container being placed on the ground and hidden by planting or partially or wholly buried. The plant growing in it can thus be made to be part of a border, which is surprisingly (if not surreally) effective with tropical plants, such as bananas and daturas (*Brugmansia* spp.), which we do not normally expect to find flourishing in among plantings of hardy shrubs or perennials. Because many conservatory plants stay much healthier outside – whitefly and redspider mite do not flourish in summer breezes and showers – this is a sensible, as well as imaginative, use of large exotica. Pots of lilies or other plants that are perhaps unattractively leggy standing on their own can be used to bring instant life to borders in this way too. The only proviso with this approach is that you do have to remember to water the container-bound plants regularly!

Choosing Plants for Containers – Practicalities

So far we have looked on the bright side of growing plants in containers. But there are disadvantages. One is that these plants are completely dependent on the gardener for water and for nutrients. Automatic watering systems exist for containers, but they tend to involve lots of plastic hose, which is unsightly, even though such arrangements can be very useful for periods when there will be no one around to water if you are going to be away on holiday. Feeding container plants is much easier now that slow-release

in containers can be moved temporarily to provide a bit of drama or colour for a party or special event. Strongly architectural plants, such as cordyline, standard bay or *Fatsia japonica*, can be moved around to provide structure to wherever it is most needed. A permanently placed standard or other formally clipped specimen is also frequently used to make a focal point.

Containers themselves are often worth admiring as works of art in their own right, deserving to be placed somewhere where they can be appreciated and complemented by appropriate planting. They make excellent focal fertilizers are available. These pellets release nutrients into the compost at a rate dependent upon temperature, more or less as and when the plants require them.

Another disadvantage of containers is that they leave the root system of a plant very exposed to the elements, whether it is getting very hot in summer or cold in winter. The classic (indeed rather clichéd) New Zealand cabbage palm (*Cordyline australis*) in an urn is so vulnerable to frost that it is best being taken out every winter. It is advisable to insulate containers by wrapping them in bubble plastic or packing them close together and stuffing the gaps between the pots with straw. Those plants that prefer a semi-shaded environment, such as camellias and rhododendrons, should be kept out of the sun to prevent the root systems getting overheated.

Plants vary greatly in their tolerance of containers. Some have a very extensive and deep-thrusting root system, which means that they can be used in containers for only one or two seasons before they become lacklustre. Most roses are quite unsuitable for long-term container planting for this reason, as are most members of the mallow family, such as hibiscus and abutilon, and the brightly coloured half-hardy sages such as *Salvia elegans* 'Scarlet Pineapple' (syn. *S. rutilans*). In fact, abutilons and half-hardy sages, like many rapidly growing half-hardy plants, can be so easily propagated from cuttings that they can be renewed every few years if not every year.

TREES AND SHRUBS

The size of tree that can be accommodated in the average container is, of course, limited, so perhaps 'tree like' might be a better term, as many shrubs can be trained as standards with a single stem and so look like a tree. Such tree-like standards are very useful in permanent collections of container plants and are greatly appreciated in roof gardens and on balconies.

A shallow rooting system is the main prerequisite for woody plants to be a success when grown in a tub or pot. Rhododendrons, azaleas, camellias and daphnes can all perform very well. Hollies (*Ilex* spp.), most conifers and birches will also thrive. Box (*Buxus* spp.) is a favourite container plant, for not only does it have a shallow rooting system but it can be easily clipped to shape.

Growing Bay Trees as Standards

Bay (*Laurus nobilis*) is probably more frequently seen grown as a standard than it is growing naturally, and it is certainly more often trained in this way than any other shrub. In fact, however, most shrubs can be made into standards.

Select the strongest stem of a young, multi-stemmed shrub, and cut off the other stems at the base. Cut off any side shoots and tie the remaining stem to a cane to encourage it to grow vertically. Continue to remove side shoots until it reaches the desired height for the development of the top. When the stem has thickened, the cane can be removed. The top will need careful attention to keep it round and even, with regular cutting back to encourage side shoots to develop. Remember to turn it around regularly so that all sides receive the same amount of light.

Lovers of rhododendrons and other lime-hating plants who live on alkaline soils will probably have realized by now what a wonderful coincidence it is that they do so well in containers, because growing them like this is far and away the best way to keep them isolated from the ground that prevents them from being a success in the garden.

CLIMBERS

Climbers may not be the obvious choice for containers, but if you can grow them free-standing in the garden, why not in a pot? Many, it is true, do not necessarily thrive, but clematis and ivies do, provided that their roots can be kept cool. They can also be used to provide living screens on balconies. Climbers can be grown as trailers, too, and allowed to cascade down, which can be very useful on balconies or steps.

Careful and regular pruning will be needed to make sure that the plants do not become a tangled mess or extend outwards to grab hold of surrounding shrubs or fittings. Because a climber in a pot tends to be inherently unstable, it is vital that the container is a heavy one, filled with a soil-based compost to provide stability.

Clematis make surprisingly good container plants, if pruned and fed regularly. The hostas' cool shades complement the pink *Clematis montana*.

Obelisks are popular and a good way of tying in a climber to maintain a formal presence.

Trellis is ideal for encouraging a more two-dimensional display.

Wigwams of canes or, for a more rustic look, of twigs, are an easy and cheap method, with the canes kept together at the top by a pot or purpose-made finial.

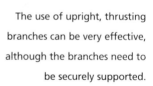

The use of upright, thrusting branches can be very effective, although the branches need to be securely supported.

Climbers with a very dense habit of growth, such as ivies (*Hedera* spp.), can be trained up wire mesh supports to make columns or whatever other shapes you wish.

PERENNIALS

Many perennials and dwarf shrubs, such as heathers and rock rose (*Cistus* spp.), do well in containers, although the larger, more rapidly growing, late-season perennials do need large pots, to provide both room for roots and stability. Perennials that spread or build up clumps may well run out of space rapidly, needing frequent division.

BULBS AND ROCKERY PLANTS

These two are almost tailormade for containers. Bulbs will transform the dullest urban environment in no time, and they mix well with other plants. As in the open garden, however, their yellowing leaves must not be removed to allow them to build up strength for next year. Those, like tulips, that need a summer baking, will get this more readily than in the ground. If necessary, most can be removed and replanted every year if it is not feasible to keep them in the pots once their leaves have died down.

Rockery plants nearly always do well in containers, and when they are combined with dwarf bulbs they can be used to make wonderfully colourful miniature gardens for late-winter and early-spring colour, enlivening window boxes and other confined spaces.

ANNUALS AND HALF-HARDY PLANTS

These are far and away the most popular container plants, and there is an ever-increasing range of varieties on the market. Every colour of the rainbow – and indeed a good many never seen in any rainbow – tinted foliage and architectural half-hardy plants are all readily available. Most are inexpensive, but for those that are not or that you fear may not be as easy to find next year, they can be easily propagated from cuttings. It is, in fact, a good idea to start taking cuttings as soon as the young plants begin to perform in early to midsummer in order to make sure that you have enough for next year. Renewing plants this way can be better than trying to keep the same ones going year after year.

Bulbs – this is *Narcissus* 'Scarlett O'Hara' – are an easy way to bring spring colour to places where a lack of soil makes conventional gardening impossible.

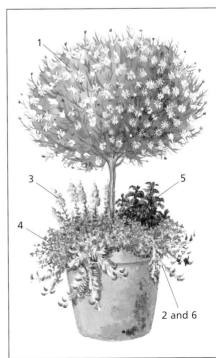

Planting containers

Because it is possible to pack large numbers of plants into containers, it is tempting to buy lots of different kinds. This is fine if the plants interest you more than anything else, but for artistic effect it is essential that you restrict the number of varieties and, of course, work to a strict colour scheme. It is helpful to think of summer container plants in several categories. Large pots can accommodate all these, and getting a balance among them that you feel happy with is the key to good container plantings.

1. A central plant, perhaps with architectural presence; this is a standard marguerite (*Argyranthemum foeniculaceum*)
2. A trailer; this is *Lotus berthelotii*
3. Theme flowers, which dominate the pot; this is pink *Diascia rigescens*
4. Secondary flowers, which complement the theme flowers; this is a little *Lobelia erinus*, which also makes a good filler plant
5. Purple or dark foliage; this is *Perilla frutescens* f. *rubra*
6. Silver foliage; *Lotus berthelotii* doubles up here

Plant Directory

Late Winter and Spring

Containerized plants seem particularly important in late winter and spring, especially for those who live in urban areas. Bulbs on their own can look rather bare, but small shrubs and perennials will help to fill out space.

Ajuga reptans
'Catlin's Giant'
- Trailing perennial
- 10 x 30cm (4 x 12in)
- Large, glossy bronze leaves and blue flowers are a good accompaniment to bulbs, especially blues and yellows. This bugle will need annual thinning because of its spreading habit.
- Grow in sun or shade.

Muscari
(grape hyacinth)
- Bulb
- 15 x 6cm (6 x 2½in)
- The intense blue of grape hyacinths together with their small size makes them ideal for small containers. Their colour combines well with smaller narcissi.
- Grow in sun; well-drained compost is essential.

Narcissi
(daffodil)
- Bulb
- Daffodils come in all shapes and sizes. There are many smaller species and varieties suitable for confined spaces, some of the smallest of which, such as the 15cm (6in) tall N. bulbocodium or N. cyclamineus, have a very distinct flower shape. Because flowering time varies considerably, from late winter to late spring, it pays to research your daffodils thoroughly and buy from a mail order specialist.
- Grow in sun or light shade.

Viburnum tinus
(laurustinus)
- Evergreen shrub
- 3 x 3m (10 x 10ft) if grown in the open ground
- Very early pink-white flowers and a compact evergreen habit make

this a most useful container shrub. Careful pruning (in spring) and regular feeding will ensure that it lasts for years. It can also be clipped to shape and pruned hard to rejuvenate it if necessary.
- Grow in sun; insulate the container during severe frosts.

Viola
- Clump-forming, short-lived perennials
- 15 x 25cm (6 x 10in) average
- Since most bulbs tend to be upright, some bushy plants that can trail over the edge are useful in spring container plantings. Violas come in all shapes, sizes and colours, from the large-flowered 'pansies' to tiny wild species. The cottage-garden-type violas tend to have a long flowering season and cover a remarkably wide colour range, including black, brown, purple, yellow, blue and red.
- Grow in sun or light shade and in fertile compost. Repropagation from cuttings after two years is usually essential.

Further suggestions
Allium spp. (onion); *Bellis* spp. (daisy); *Camellia* spp.; *Chionodoxa* spp. (glory of the snow); *Clematis alpina*; *Convallaria* spp. (lily-of-the-valley); *Corydalis* spp.; *Erysimum* spp. (syn. *Cheiranthus* spp.; wallflower); *Primula* spp.; *Scilla* spp. *Tulipa* spp. (tulip); *Vinca* spp. (periwinkle)

Summer Containers

Summer container plantings are immensely popular and should continue to be so, given the ever-increasing range of plants being introduced. For flowers all summer long, deadhead and feed regularly. Occasionally pinch out growing tips to encourage bushiness.

Antirrhinum
'Black Prince'
- Perennial
- 40 x 30cm (16 x 12in)
- There is nothing like black (very dark purple, actually) to create interest and focus attention like this variety of snapdragon. It looks good with pale pinks and with silver or cream foliage.
- Grow in sun. Bring it indoors in winter or propagate annually.

Argyranthemum foeniculaceum
(syn. *A.* 'Silver Queen'; marguerite)

- Evergreen perennial
- 1 x 1m (3 x 3ft)
- White and yellow daisies stand out against a background of finely divided grey foliage. It is ideal for a large container, but can be trained into a standard.
- Grow in sun. It is scarcely hardy, so bring indoors over winter.

Brachyscome iberidifolia
(Swan River daisy)

- Annual
- 40 x 40cm (16 x 16in)
- Mauve-blue daisies are borne over fine quite dark foliage. Pink, mauve and white forms are also available. It has a bushy, slightly trailing habit, and is a good filler among larger and stiffer plants.
- Grow in sun.

Diascia

- Spreading, short-lived perennials
- 30 x 50cm (12 x 20in)
- Unknown a few years ago, diascias are now deservedly popular plants, with varieties producing flowers in dozens of shades of

pink. All have a somewhat floppy, semi-trailing habit. *D. rigescens* has a more definite habit than most, with flowers in tight heads. *D. fetcaniensis* is the hardiest for general garden use.

- Grow in sun and in fertile soil. Protect over winter and propagate some more every year to be sure you keep them.

Felicia amelloides
(syn. *Agathea coelestis*, *Aster capensis*; blue marguerite)

- Evergreen perennial
- 40 x 60cm (16 x 24in)
- One of the best summer blues, these daisy flowers are borne on a bushy plant, which complements taller plants. It looks good with silver or cream foliage and with either pinks or yellows.
- Not hardy, but worth treating as a winter-flowering conservatory plant.

Further suggestions

Alonsoa spp.; *Calendula* spp. (marigold); *Cleome* spp. (spider flower); *Impatiens* spp. (busy lizzie); *Lilium* spp. (lily); *Lobelia* spp.; *Nemesia* spp.; *Nicotiana* spp. (tobacco plant); *Osteospermum* spp; *Pelargonium* spp.; *Penstemon* spp. (beard-tongue); *Petunia* cultivars; *Sphaeralcea* spp.; *Tagetes* spp. (marigold); *Verbena* spp.

Foliage in Containers
Attractive or coloured foliage in containers not only complements the flowers but provides interest at times when the flowers are few and far between.

Hosta

- Herbaceous perennial
- 30 x 40cm (12 x 16in) average, producing flower spikes up to 80cm (32in)
- Hostas, in particular the elegant blue-grey-leaved *H. sieboldiana* var. *elegans*, make good container plants for shaded locations, perhaps combined with ferns or other shade-tolerant, leafy plants.
- Grow in fertile compost; regular watering is essential. Hostas are very hardy.

Diascia integerrima

Hosta sieboldiana 'Elegans'

Lotus berthelotii
(parrot's beak)

- Evergreen perennial
- 80cm (32in) trailing
- Although the scarlet lobster-claw flowers, borne in early summer, are quite spectacular, it is the fine silver foliage that makes this a good companion to strongly coloured pinks and blues in containers and, especially, hanging baskets. Easily propagated from cuttings, it is worth keeping as a winter conservatory plant.
- Never allow it to dry out or it will lose its leaves. It is not hardy.

Perilla frutescens f. rubra

- Annual
- 60 x 30cm (24 x 12in)
- The red-purple leaves with a distinct aroma can be used in salads. It has a compact habit, and it combines well with pinks and blues.
- Plant out after the last frosts and grow in sun.

Senecio cineraria
(syn. *S. maritimus*)

- Evergreen shrub
- 30 x 30cm (12 x 12in)
- The very silver, deeply cut leaves are a classic accompaniment to summer bedding. It has a bushy habit, so goes well with trailing plants, and looks good with all colours except yellow.
- Grow in sun. It is almost hardy.

Silybum marianum
(Blessed Mary's thistle)

- Biennial
- 10 x 20cm (4 x 8in)
- Fine silver veining on a rosette of leaves make this a distinctive container plant, especially when grown alongside less exotic herbs, wildflowers and perennials.
- Discard after the first year.

Further suggestions
Atriplex hortensis var. *rubra* (red mountain spinach); *Brassica oleracea* (ornamental cabbage); *Helichrysum splendidum*; *Milium effusum* 'Aureum'; *Ocimum basilicum* var. *purpurascens* (basil)

Permanent Container Plants
Permanent containers are vital for those with no gardens. They can feature the following plants and many others alongside bulbs and temporary spring plants, such as violas. Provided that planting and end-of-season removal does not cause too much root disturbance, summer plants can be grown with them, too.

Carex testacea

- Evergreen grass-like plant
- 40 x 25cm (16 x 10in)
- Golden-green arching leaves in neat tufts make this a very handy all-year container plant, useful as a centrepiece to smaller varieties.
- Grow in sun or very light shade.

Erica carnea
(syn. *E. herbacea*; alpine heath, winter heath)

- Evergreen dwarf shrub
- 30 x 40cm (12 x 16in)
- Winter-flowering heathers are a godsend to those who have no garden to cultivate, because they make excellent container plants and tolerate alkaline compost and water. Not only is there an enormous range of varieties, from deep red-pink to white, but some have yellow- or orange-tinged foliage.
- Grow in sun or light shade. Good drainage is essential, but never allow the compost to dry out. Clip hard after flowering.

Hebe
'Red Edge'

- Evergreen shrub
- 50 x 50cm (20 x 20in)
- A neat habit and grey leaves tinged with pink make this a very useful container plant. Use as a centrepiece, but make sure that it is not hemmed in, or it will lose its distinct habit.
- Grow in sun.

Ophiopogon planiscarpus
'Nigrescens'
- Evergreen perennial
- 15 x 30cm (6 x 12in)
- Almost black leaves on a plant that resembles a grass. Good for smaller containers as a contrast to lighter or brighter colours.
- Grow in sun.

Pyracantha
'Orange Glow'
- Evergreen shrub
- 4.5 x 3m (15 x 10ft) in open ground
- Bright orange berries last until well into the winter on a dense shrub that can be easily clipped to shape or trained close to a trellis. Cream flowers appear in spring.
- Grow in sun or light shade.

Further suggestions

Acer palmatum dwarf varieties; *Agapanthus* spp; *Alyssum* spp.; *Aubrieta* spp.; *Buxus* spp. (box); *Camellia* spp.; *Daphne* spp.; *Erica* spp.; *Festuca* spp. (fescue); *Fuchsia* spp.; *Hebe* spp. (shrubby veronica); *Hedera* spp. (ivy); *Ilex* spp. (holly); *Jasminum nudiflorum* (winter jasmine); *Kalmia latifolia* (calico bush); *Lamium* spp. (deadnettle); *Laurus* spp. (bay, laurel); *Lavandula* spp. (lavender); *Leptospermum* spp.; *Pieris* spp.; *Pittosporum* spp.; *Yucca* spp.; dwarf conifers, rockery plants

Dual Use Conservatory/Garden Plants
Conservatory plants often stay healthier if put outside in summer. The following can be stood outside in their pots or planted out in borders, to be potted up and brought inside in winter. Warm, sheltered spots in full sun and plentiful water and feeding are vital for success.

Abutilon
- Evergreen shrubs
- 2 x 1m (6 x 3ft) one season's growth
- There are seemingly endlessly produced red, yellow, orange, white or pink flowers. Abutilon grows rapidly once planted out in a border but it may not take kindly to being dug up again. Propagation from cuttings is very easy, though.

Brugmansia arborea
(syn. *Datura arborea, D. cornigera*; angel's trumpet)
- Evergreen shrub
- 2 x 1m (6 x 3ft) one season's growth
- Huge, cream, pendant trumpets have the most fantastic fragrance at night. Rapid and greedy grower – use tomato fertilizer.

Solanum rantonnetii
(blue potato bush)
- Evergreen shrub
- 1.5 x 0.7m (5ft x 28in) one season's growth
- Deep mauve, yellow-centred 'potato flowers' are borne all summer long on a somewhat wildly ranging branching shrub. It is good for combining with larger summer seasonal plants, such as felicias, salvias and argyranthemums.

Sollya heterophylla
(syn. *S. fusiformis*; bluebell creeper)
- Evergreen climber
- 2 x 0.5m (6ft x 20in) ultimately
- Small, pure blue flowers are carried all summer long on a twining climber, which is suitable for smaller scale plantings with other blue and mauve flowers or with silver foliage. It is not especially vigorous and easily maintained in a container.
- Grow in sun or light shade. It will survive very light frosts.

Further suggestions

Anisodontea spp.; *Citrus* spp.; *Cuphea* spp.; *Nerium* spp.; *Olea* spp.; *Plumbago* spp.; *Salvia* spp. (sage); *Tibouchina* spp.

Brugmansia arborea

'Instant' gardens

There is no such thing as an 'instant' garden; plants are not like machines that will give satisfaction as soon as they are bought. There are, however, a number of short cuts to transforming gardens for those who simply can't wait, perhaps because they have to hide ugly surroundings or a special event is to be celebrated in the garden, or simply because they are impatient. One way is just to buy large plants (often referred to as 'specimen' plants). Another is to use varieties that establish and grow quickly.

Big Plants – Now!

Increasing numbers of nurseries and garden centres are specializing in larger than normal sizes of commonly available trees, shrubs and climbers, often confusingly termed 'specimen-sized plants'. There are a number of drawbacks to buying such plants, however. One is that they are often grown in a warmer climate than the one in which they are sold and planted, and may not be hardened off to survive colder winters than they are used to. Another is that they simply do not establish so well, especially if pot grown. Indeed, younger plants put in at the same time may catch up after several years. Moreover, drought will do far more damage to a newly planted shrub that is 1m (3ft) high than to one that has had a couple of years in which to get its roots right down to the deeper and moister layers of soil.

The greatest drawback is, perhaps, the investment of money and time in plants that may fail or that may turn out to be wrongly named. If, however, you do wish to go

Above: A selection of bulbs, perennials and biennials will create a border full of colour in less than two years, with many looking good in their first year.

along this path, it is advisable to concentrate on those varieties that are more or less guaranteed to succeed, those that are known to be easy and vigorous and, of course, those that you know will thrive in the conditions your garden offers. In addition, you may wish to buy in large specimens of varieties that are slow to establish (although they will often be more expensive as a consequence). Wisterias, which can take many years before they flower, rhododendrons, which are slow, and palms – the very hardy windmill fan (*Trachycarpus fortunei*) only! – which grow faster in the warmer climates where they are grown commercially, are all examples of plants with which this might be worth doing.

Specimen plants need sites in which the soil has been carefully prepared, because the roots will have youthful vigour to go questing into spaces new. Trees and taller shrubs will need stout staking, because their root systems will take several years to grow sufficiently to anchor them against wind rock. All will need thorough irrigation in periods of dry weather, preferably by means of water that is directed at the rootball via a pipe.

Given the financial investment in using specimen plants, it may be worthwhile spending a little more and getting

professional help with the planting. They weigh an awful lot, and often the very act of planting them is a job for several strong people.

Quick Results with Quick Plants

Cheaper and more natural than using large plants is to use quick-growing ones. You are limited in what you can grow, but if a garden full of growth and greenery is more important than one full of particular species, then this is the route to take.

Herbaceous perennials – those that renew all their above-ground growth every year – establish rapidly, much more quickly than woody plants like trees and shrubs. After three years a perennial can often look as if it has been in place for ten. Herbaceous perennials are most useful for filling out horizontal space, especially if they are listed as being good ground-cover plants. Dying back to ground level every winter, they are not as good for filling vertical space, however. Because most flower the first year they are planted, they are extremely useful for pretty well instant colour.

Bulbs are another good way to bring instant colour to a garden, especially because so many are so vivid. The majority flower in spring, but summer-flowering bulbs, such as lilies (*Lilium* spp.), are worth remembering too. Bulbs have little bulk, however, and so their use in the 'instant' garden is limited to providing colour. It should be borne in mind that many do not reliably flower again after the first year or two, tulips in particular, and if you are looking beyond the first year, go for daffodils and narcissi, snowdrops (*Galanthus* spp.), crocuses, grape hyacinths (*Muscari* spp.) and scillas.

Of the taller growing and bulkier plants, the most rapid-growing are generally the climbers, such as honeysuckle (*Lonicera* spp.), clematis and the various vines grown for their foliage, such as the virginia creeper (*Parthenocissus*

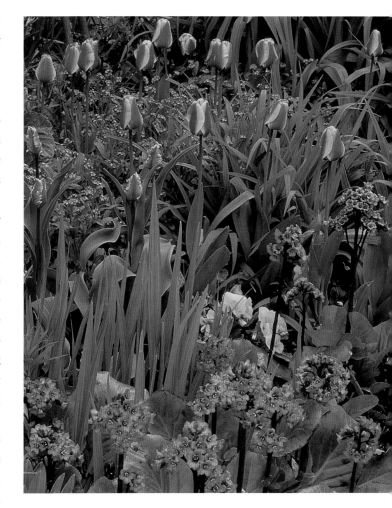

Bulbs are the most reliable form of instant planting. The evergreen perennial bergenia in the foreground will take two years to begin to look established.

quinquefolia). New gardens with lots of bare walls and dull, mass-produced fencing can be transformed in three years by means of climbers. Their use need not be restricted to pre-existing vertical surfaces. If getting in lots of upright-growing plants is important to you, you must provide more supports for free-standing climbers. Ready-made obelisks and other supports are readily available in

Free-standing supports for climbers are one of the best ways to create instant impact in the garden

An off-the-peg, ready-made obelisk

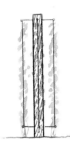

A fence-post with wires attached and held taut by vine eyes to the top and bottom; this is most effective if done on all four sides

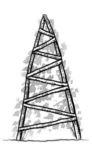

A rustic-style, three-sided support made from branches and twigs fixed by nails

An off-the-peg metal support, particularly suited to roses due to its strength. These are easy to have made from steel reinforcing rods by anyone with access to basic welding equipment

wood and metal, but they are expensive and increasingly look clichéd. We've all seen too many of them in the gardens of chic designers. Get out the hammer and nails and make your own.

A number of very fast climbers can become very big; they should be regarded with the same suspicion as poplars and eucalyptus. Russian vine (*Fallopia baldschuanica*, syn. *Polygonum baldschuanicum*) is the most notorious,

Clematis montana, always a rapid grower, is here running along what used to be a washing line!

reaching 18m (60ft) eventually and 5–6m (16–20ft) after five years. It is just the thing for covering large eyesores, but not for quickly covering a fence! Its other common name is the mile-a-minute plant. The kiwi fruit (*Actinidia deliciosa*; syn. *A. chinensis*) and crimson glory vine (*Vitis coignetiae*) grow at about a half to two-thirds that speed to reach a similar eventual size but are much more majestic plants, and the vine has superb autumn colour. Of flowering climbers, the pink *Clematis montana* and the honeysuckles *Lonicera periclymenum* and *L. japonica* are easily the fastest growing.

Trees and shrubs vary greatly in their speed of growth. Those that grow the fastest often do so for many years to come, ending up perhaps far bigger than you ever intended, which can be a major embarrassment. So, if you are not to overshadow the entire neighbourhood, make sure you know how large your selected trees are to going to get. Of all fast-growing trees, perhaps the birches are the most useful. They do not get too large – 12 × 5m (40 × 16ft) at most – all are beautiful and elegant trees, and the shade they cast is relatively light. Willows (*Salix* spp.) also grow fast, as do serviceberry trees (*Amelanchier* spp.) and rowans (*Sorbus* spp.).

Of large trees that take off rapidly, we have mentioned several in the chapter on Specimen Plants (see page 60).

It is also worth mentioning poplars (*Populus* spp.), perhaps as a warning if nothing else. They may make very good windbreaks but do grow very large, very fast, are not particularly attractive and are disease prone. One of the major topics in the village in which I live is one person's line of poplars, which blocks the view of a whole row of houses. Eucalyptus grow very fast, too. Although they are certainly attractive, they are also all too frequently carelessly planted. Quite apart from the vast size they can reach, they never look quite right in many traditional settings.

Shrubs are grown not just for their flowers, but for their bulk: they occupy space in the garden. This bulk is, of course, more attractive if it is made up of interesting foliage. Far too many rapidly growing shrubs have rather dull foliage, however, and an all too short flowering season. Small gardens cannot afford to waste space in this way. If fast-growing, woody plants are needed in a garden there must be good reason for growing them other than their ability to fill space quickly.

An example of the kind of shrub needed for rapid effect would be the ceanothus. They grow quickly, and have reasonably attractive foliage and stunning blue flowers in early summer; they are, however, not hardy in very cold areas. Buddleias, if you are certain that you have space for a 4×4m (13×13ft) shrub, also grow extremely fast, and they can be cut back to the base every few years to restrict their size.

Wetland plants are often very fast growing, but only if your soil is actually moist all summer long. It follows that a pond or bog garden is a feature that, although it might take effort to build, will, once made, produce rapid results.

Annuals for Instant Colour

If bulbs are the solution for instant spring colour, it is annuals that can fulfil this role in summer. More than any other category of plants, these are the choice of many gardeners for floral displays. Many flower for several months from midsummer until the first frosts, with the minimum of effort on the part of the gardener, making them ideal for new gardens, where they can fill the gaps between newly planted perennials and shrubs. Because they live for only one year, their remains can be removed with a minimum of effort once they have died back.

Ceanothus – this is *C. arboreus* 'Trewithen Blue' – are some of the finest shrubs that grow really fast, making a cloud of blue in early summer.

Hardy annuals can be sown as seed straight into the ground. Many have cottage-garden associations and a soft, romantic appearance. Half-hardy annuals, often called bedding plants, are from warmer climes and need to be grown from seed under glass before being planted out after the last frosts. They have a bad name with many gardeners because of their associations with garish public displays and the ill-proportioned nature of many of the plants that is the result of intensive breeding. The usefulness of plants that can be bought, planted out and be flowering within weeks cannot be denied, however, and the choice of half-hardy plants has increased rapidly over recent years, with many of the new species having subtler colours and a more natural form than the mass market favourites.

Those who garden with foresight may choose to sow seeds of annuals in spring to fill out the gaps in their new garden or newly redeveloped area. Those who are less organized may achieve instant planting with the bedding plants available from garden centres a month or two later. The options for temporarily filling space in gardens with almost instant colour have never been greater.

While most annuals are small, some do get to an enormous size with remarkable speed, making them truly invaluable for filling up space in a few months: sunflowers (*Helianthus annuus*) are the best known but castor oil plant (*Ricinus communis*) (note, the seeds are highly toxic) and varieties of amaranthus get quite substantial, too.

The instant garden in late summer

1. Russian vine (*Fallopia baldschuanica*, syn. *Polygonum baldschuanicum*) runs up training wires fixed to the sides of the garage. It will eventually run over the top to conceal it

2. Climbers are fixed to wires attached to fencing: honeysuckle (*Lonicera periclymenum*), *Clematis montana*, *C. orientalis* and ivy (*Hedera colchica*)

3. Climbers grow up trellis as an alternative and faster screening than a hedge: *Clematis armandii* and honeysuckle (*Lonicera japonica* 'Halliana')

4. A free-standing, half-hardy climber, the cup-and-saucer vine (*Cobaea scandens*) grows as an annual, running up branches stuck vertically into the ground

5. Summer-flowering bulbs: lilies (*Lilium regale* and *L.* 'Amber Gold')

6. Summer-flowering tuberous plants: *Dahlia* 'Athalie'

7. Containers of annuals and half-hardy plants: pelargonium and petunia varieties, *Perilla frutescens* f. *rubra* and *Brachyscome iberidifolia*

8. Large annuals: castor oil plant (*Ricinus communis*) and sunflowers (*Helianthus annuus*)

9. Half-hardy perennials: *Argyranthemum foeniculaceum*, *A.* 'Jamaica Primrose' and *A.* 'Vancouver', varieties of diascia, osteospermum and penstemon, and *Felicia amelloides* 'Santa Anita'

10. Herbaceous perennials: *Eupatorium purpureum* 'Atropurpureum', *Solidago* 'Lemore', *Aster novae-angliae* and *A.* x *frikartii* varieties, and *Geranium* x *oxonianum* varieties

11. Hardy annuals sown *in situ*: cornflower (*Centaurea cyanus*), *Phacelia tanacetifolia*, *Nigella* 'Persian Jewels', opium poppy (*Papaver somniferum*), poached-egg plant (*Limnanthes douglasii*) and tickseed (*Coreopsis tinctoria*)

12. Fast-growing tree: walnut (*Juglans regia*)

13. Fast-growing shrub: *Ceanothus impressus*

14. Pond with waterside plants: *Acorus calamus* 'Variegatus', *Houttuynia cordata* 'Chameleon' and *Pontedaria cordata*

15. Moisture-loving plants in associated boggy area: *Rheum palmatum* 'Atrosanguineum' and *Darmera peltata*

Plant Directory

Fast-growing Shrubs

A new garden needs filling out fast. These are among the fastest attractive shrubs for doing just that.

Buddleja
(buddleia)

- Deciduous shrubs
- 4 x 4m (13 x 13ft)
- Densely packed flower spikes, attractive to butterflies, make buddleias popular, and they are among the fastest growing of garden shrubs. The most familiar is *B. davidii*, with varieties with flowers in shades of purple, but there are others, such as the yellow *B. globosa*. Pruning extends the life of the plant.
- Plant in sun and in any reasonable soil, including those that are dry and poor.

Ceanothus

- Evergreen shrubs
- 4 x 4m (13 x 13ft)
- Most varieties of this shrub produce masses of blue flowers in early summer, although some, such as *C.* 'Autumnal Blue', flower later. Their dark evergreen foliage is attractive, too. Ceanothus are not hardy in very cold areas, being damaged by hard frosts and cold wind. *C. thrysiflorus* and *C. impressus* are among the hardiest.
- Plant in full sun and in any reasonable soil, including those that are poor and dry.

Cotoneaster x *watereri*
'Cornubia'

- Evergreen shrub
- 7 x 7m (23 x 23ft)
- Of the numerous varieties of cotoneaster, the larger growing ones are notably fast growers, including *C.* x *watereri* 'Cornubia', which is evergreen, bearing a good display of red berries in autumn, as, indeed, do most cotoneasters. *C. simonsii* is a similar species but is semi-evergreen.

Escallonia

- Evergreen shrubs
- 3 x 3m (10 x 10ft)
- The glossy leaves are a good backdrop to red flowers, although some varieties, such as *E.* 'Apple Blossom', are pink and others, such as *E.* 'Iveyi', are white.
- Grow in sun or light shade and in any reasonable soil. Escallonia does best in mild maritime localities, so protect it from cold winds. It can be used for hedging.

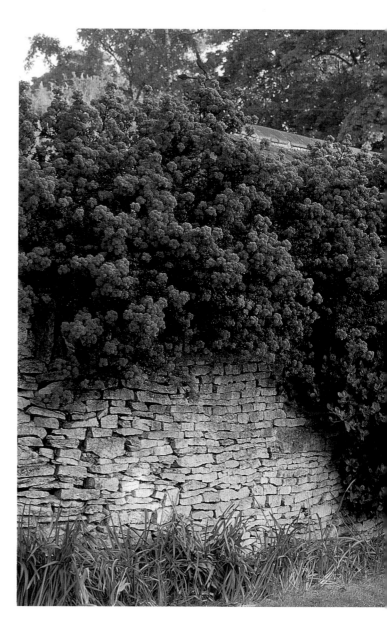

Ceanothus impressus

Kolkwitzia amabalis
(beauty bush)

- Deciduous shrub
- 3 x 3m (10 x 10ft)
- A shrub with most attractive soft pink flowers in late spring, it is not as fast growing as cotoneaster or escallonia, but it is still relatively quick.
- Grow in sun or light shade and in any reasonable soil.

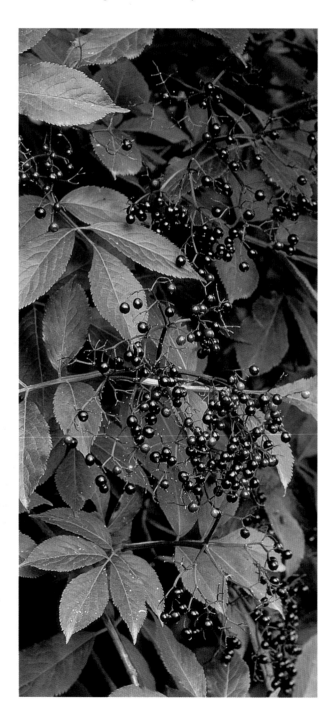

Sambucus nigra
(common elder)

- Deciduous shrub
- 6 x 5m (20 x 16ft)
- Available in various decorative forms, the common elder is a notably rapid grower. *S. n.* 'Aurea' has yellowish foliage; *S. n.* 'Guincho Purple' (syn. *S. n.* 'Purpurea') has purple foliage; while *S. n.* f. *laciniata* has heavily divided leaves. Once established, hard cutting back every few years encourages the shrub to produce the most attractive foliage.
- Grow in sun to medium shade and any soil, including wet ones.

Further suggestions

Cornus alba (red-barked dogwood), *C. stolonifera* (red osier dogwood); *Forsythia* spp.; *Genista aetnensis* (Mount Etna broom); *Hydrangea macrophylla*; *Lavatera olbia*; *Ligustrum lucidum* (Chinese privet); *Lonicera nitida* (box-leaved honeysuckle), *L. pileata*; *Philadelphus* spp. (mock orange); *Pyracantha* spp.; *Rosa glauca*, *R. rugosa* and many other large shrub roses; *Spartium* spp.; *Spiraea* spp.; *Photinia* spp. (syn. *Stranvaesia* spp.)

Instant Perennials

Almost all perennials grow relatively quickly, with the later flowering tall species notably fast to establish. The following is a selection of those that bulk up especially quickly, to help the garden look mature as soon as possible.

Helenium
(sneezeweed)

- Spreading, clump-forming perennials
- 1.5 x 0.5m (5ft x 20in)
- Flowers in shades of yellow, red and brown top tall stems in late summer, so sneezeweed goes well with the flower colours of most other late-season perennials.
- Grow in sun and in any reasonable soil. Division is beneficial every few years, but if you have more space to fill, a few more (free!) plants will not go amiss.

Sambucus nigra

Helianthus

'Lemon Queen'

- Spreading, clump-forming perennial
- 1.5 x 0.5m (5ft x 20in)
- Lovely primrose-pale yellow flowers set this autumn daisy well apart from all its brighter cousins. It is perfect for combining with blue and violet asters.
- Grow in sun and any fertile soil.

Leucanthemum × *superbum*

(syn. *Chrysanthemum maximum*; shasta daisy)

- Spreading, clump-forming perennial
- 90 x 50cm (36 x 20in)
- This familiar perennial has yellow-centred, big white daisies. It grows well on most soils, but does need fertility to perform well. It is not always long lived.
- Grow in full sun.

Persicaria

(knotweed)

- Clump-forming herbaceous perennials
- Cousins of the infamous Japanese knotweed, many of these plants are vigorous but do not have the same terrifying speed of spread. Early summer-flowering *P. bistorta* 'Superba', 60 x 80cm (24 x 32in), has soft pink flowers and can certainly grow fast, but only seriously on damp soils. *P. amplexicaulis*, 1.2 x 1.2m (4 x 4ft), is not really a spreader, but it is a most useful late-summer bulky perennial with pink 'rat-tail' flowers. *P. polymorphum*, 1.5 x 1.5m (5 x 5ft), is set to become one of the best big border plants of all time: non-spreading with cream flowers all summer long.
- Grow in sun and any reasonable soil, but preferably not dry.

Solidago

(golden rod)

- Spreading herbaceous perennials
- 1.5 x 0.6m (5 x 2ft)
- A rather down-market image stops many gardeners from making more use of these autumn flowers, whose plumes of gold consort well with purple asters. Superior varieties, such as *S.* 'Goldenmosa', 1.00 x 0.6m (3 x 2ft), which grow well but not excessively, are well worth it.
- Grow in sun and in any reasonable soil.

Further suggestions

Aster spp.; *Cephalaria gigantea* (syn. *C. tatarica*); *Echinops* spp. (globe thistle); *Eupatorium purpureum* (Joe Pye weed); *Filipendula* spp. (meadowsweet); *Geranium* spp.; *Inula* spp.; *Macleaya* spp. (plume poppy); *Polygonum* spp.; *Rheum* spp. (ornamental rhubarb); *Rudbeckia laciniata*; *Verbascum* spp.

Helenium 'Moerheim Beauty'

Clematis montana

Quick Climbers

Climbers that grow fast are much needed to cover bare walls, fences or eyesores.

Akebia quinata
(chocolate vine)

- Deciduous twining climber
- 6 x 6m (20 x 20ft)
- The attractive leaves are divided into five leaflets and fragrant maroon-purple flowers are borne in spring. The whole plant is vaguely exotic in appearance.
- It grows best in light shade and in any reasonable soil.

Clematis montana

- Deciduous climber
- 10 x 10m (33 x 33ft)
- Smothered in pink flowers in early summer, this very large-growing and popular clematis is familiar to most gardeners. Various varieties offer a colour range from white to deep pink. It requires support and, like all clematis, needs its head in the sun and its feet in the shade.
- Plant in any soil that is not too dry.

Clematis orientalis, C. tangutica

- Deciduous climber
- 5 x 5m (16 x 16ft)
- Two practically identical clematis, with most unusual thick, yellow petals borne in late summer to early autumn. There are silvery, hairy seedheads in early winter.
- Grow in any soil that is not too dry.

Lonicera periclymenum
(common honeysuckle)

- Deciduous climber
- 6 x 6m (20 x 20ft)
- This well-known, highly fragrant, yellow-flowered climber blooms in summer. *L. p.* 'Belgica' flowers in early summer; *L. p.* 'Graham Thomas' and 'Serotina' flower in midsummer to autumn. The plants need support.
- Grow in sun or light shade; deep, rich, moist but well-drained soil is vital for good results.

Rosa
(large rambling roses)

- Deciduous climbers
- to 10 x 10m (33 x 33ft)
- If you have lots of space to fill, such as a strong mature tree,

then these are the most majestic of climbers. In the wrong place they can overwhelm or crush their supports. Huge-growing varieties like R. 'Francis E. Lester' and R. 'Rambling Rector' flower once, but spectacularly, in early summer, but there are smaller ones, such as R. multiflora and R. moschata. Most have single flowers in white and various shades of pink.

• Grow in sun to medium shade and in deep, fertile soil.

Further suggestions

Actinidia deliciosa (syn. *A. chinensis*; kiwi fruit); *Aristolochia macrophylla*; *Clematis armandii*; *Lonicera* x *americana*, *L. japonica* (Japanese honeysuckle); *Passiflora caerulea* (blue passion flower); *Solanum* spp.; *Vitis* spp. (vine)

Annuals for a Splash

Annuals are somehow quintessentially 'summer', and what better way to fill in the gaps in a new planting scheme to make an impact the first season? The majority of annuals do best on a soil that is not too rich, which encourages flowering. A long flowering season depends on their being thinned out, giving each plant plenty of space, and in removing dead flowers where possible (deadheading).

All the following are hardy annuals – that is, they may be sown in spring directly in the positions in which they are to flower.

Centaurea cyanus
(cornflower)
• Annual
• 90 x 30cm (3 x 1ft)
• Bright blue flowers on tall stems distinguish the cornflower, but there are varieties with pink, white and even black-purple flowers.
• Grow in sun and in any reasonable soil.

Clarkia amoena
• Annual
• 60 x 30cm (2 x 1ft)
• The flowers in shades of pink, some double, some single, look best if the plants are grown *en masse*.
• Grow in sun and in any reasonable soil.

Eschscholzia californica
(California poppy)
• Annual
• 30 x 15cm (12 x 6in)
• Poppy-like flowers in shades of orange and yellow are borne above blue-tinged feathery foliage.
• Grow in sun and in any reasonable soil.

Helianthus annuus
(sunflower)
• Annual
• 3 x 0.4m (10ft x 16in)
• The well-known sunflower is a sure way to create some instant height in the garden. There is now quite a range of colours – from yellow to dark orange – and heights.
• Grow in sun and in reasonably fertile soil for good results.

Limnanthes douglasii
(poached-egg plant, meadow foam)
• Annual
• 15 x 10cm (6 x 4in)
• Yellow flowers with a white rim have given this annual its common name. Flowering all summer, it is a good gap filler.
• Grow in sun and in any reasonable soil.

Nigella damascena
(love-in-a-mist)
• Annual
• 40 x 20cm (16 x 10in)
• Blue flowers amid finely divided foliage are followed by decorative seedheads. Mixtures are available with pink and white flowers, too.
• Grow in sun and in any reasonable soil.

Further suggestions

Agrostemma githago; *Amaranthus caudatus* (love-lies-bleeding); *Calendula officinalis* (pot marigold); *Consolida ajacis* (syn. *C. ambigua*; larkspur); *Cosmos* hybrids; *Lavatera trimestris*; *Linum grandiflorum* 'Rubrum'; *Nemophila* spp.; *Omphalodes linifolia*; *Papaver rhoeas* (common poppy), *P. somniferum* (opium poppy); *Phacelia tanacetifolia*; *Rudbeckia hirta* (syn. *R. gloriosa*; black-eyed Susan); *Silene armeria*

New life
for old borders

A new garden is rarely a blank slate, as books on garden design so often seem to think. For the most part, anyone creating or developing a garden has to start from within a framework that is already largely decided for them. Although this can be a problem for the ambitious, it can also be a blessing in disguise. Mature trees in particular can never be bought off the peg (unless you are something big in Hollywood), and while they may not be in the place that you would have chosen, they are a valuable part of the garden and often the whole neighbourhood. As for features such as terraces and ponds, someone else at least has put in the money and effort to make them, saving you the task.

In this section I want to discuss in detail how to go about transforming an elderly planting; in the final chapter there is more detail on rejuvenating and transforming other garden features. Neglected borders can often look so much like gardens gone to seed, sometimes worse than waste ground. At least with the latter one can just bulldoze the lot and start again. Not knowing where to start with an old border is a major part of the problem. It helps to break the task down into bite-sized units: weeding, dealing with trees, shrubs, old perennials and bulbs, and replanting. But first we need to establish some general principles.

Give the Place a Chance to Prove Itself

An old border in the garden of a property you have just bought may contain all sorts of horrors, from nettles to

Above: Borders that take a lot of time to maintain can often be turned into 'wild borders', if robust plants are chosen. Here two centaurea species consort with astrantia and a lavender.

mint gone mad, but the chances are that it will contain all sorts of joys as well. You will never get to appreciate these if you cut everything down in one go, before waiting to see what will develop.

A well-known garden writer I know bought a new house and announced her intention not to do anything with the garden for a year. By doing this, she would learn such things as where the sun was at different times of year, where the weeds were and what plants grew where, bulbs and winter-dormant perennials in particular.

Start Gently

The best way to deal with a newly acquired old border is first to remove the top growth of all obvious weeds, simply to stop them getting any worse. Then the border can be left, allowing you to see what is growing where. Only when you are absolutely sure that you are not going to dig up some good plants, should you start on the process of wholesale weed digging.

Record What's There

Taking photographs and making a note of when they were taken is a good way of keeping tabs on what is growing where. Marking the position of bulbs and perennials that disappear over the winter with large labels is another easy way. Only the keen amateur surveyor is likely to want to map out the border.

Remember to mark things as soon as they begin to die down – some perennials, like the large-flowered poppy (*Papaver orientale*) and some dicentras, die down in midsummer, and many others, peonies for example, have leaves that disappear rapidly when they are dead. Clump-formers, like hardy geraniums, and tall-growing perennials, like phlox and asters, leave convenient stems to show their positions. Don't cut these back – they are invaluable as markers!

Weeding

This is an important task, because whatever else you decide to do with the border, you probably do not want it full of nettles and ground elder. On the other hand, you might want to leave a few of some types of weeds to feed butterfly larvae; nettles are, in fact, one of their most important food sources. In this case, a few weeds can be left in position somewhere inconspicuous, such as behind a large shrub.

The difficult thing about weeding an old border is the way in which weeds and many ornamentals get inextricably bound together, which makes hand weeding seem an almost herculean task. If the weed problem is severe, you may end up digging out all the perennials and bulbs, fishing out the weed roots and replacing them, only later, when the bed has been completely cleared. It helps to understand the weeds.

The following are the worst offenders to deal with, and are the most widespread.

BRAMBLES (*RUBUS FRUTICOSUS*)

In mild climates brambles are evergreen and grow voraciously, even over large shrubs. Fortunately, they can be relatively easily removed by digging out the base of each plant with its roots. Unlike many weeds, they do not send out irritating little roots that are easy to miss.

Those that are hopelessly intermingled with shrubs can be pulled off and the stems and leaves painted with a brushwood killer (see overleaf), which will penetrate to their roots but not affect the shrub.

GRASSES

Many grasses form a thick turf, which strangles less vigorous or winter-dormant perennials. It is often simply removed by digging out. Runners left behind by species such as couch (*Agropyron repens*) will always regenerate, and will need treatment with a glyphosate-based weed-killer (see overleaf).

GROUND ELDER (*AEGOPODIUM PODAGRARIA*)

This is one of the worst weeds to deal with, because its runners go everywhere and every little bit that is left in the ground will regenerate and form a new little plant the following spring. Its invulnerability to glyphosate and many other herbicides makes it a difficult foe. Consider the 'black plastic option' (see overleaf) or simply try to remove as much as you can and grow some of the weed-suppressant perennials in the list below.

NETTLES (*URTICA DIOICIA*)

Nettles have tough, bright yellow, interconnected roots near the surface, making them easy to dig out in satisfyingly large quantities. Survivors can be dug out the following spring. They are easily dealt with by the right herbicide, such as Ammonium sulphamate (see overleaf).

PLANTS WITH TAPROOTS

Docks (*Rumex* spp.), dandelions (*Taraxacum officinale*) and other plants with taproots can be dug out to make a good pile of roots, and then all the little deep bits that you left behind will pop back up again in the spring. These are good candidates for glyphosate or black plastic.

HORSETAIL (*EQUISETUM*)

This is a very primitive plant, immensely resilient to attempts at chemical and physical control. It favours damp ground or areas with a history of poor drainage but is easily imported in introduced soil. Because of its resistance to the weedkillers that affect other weeds, it can actually benefit from their use, because they reduce its competitors. If you plan to maintain your border with frequent traditional cultivation, such as hoeing, then it is not too much of a problem. In low-maintenance borders, however, where the soil is never disturbed, horsetail can increase prolifically, although it can be effectively shaded out by growing plants that become taller than it does, generally over 40cm (16in).

Controlling Weeds in Old Borders

If the weed problem seems pretty serious, consider using herbicides. Most herbicides designed to kill weeds do not affect shrubs and so can be safely used around them.

Glyphosate is a very safe, rapidly bio-degraded chemical that kills grass, docks, dandelions and many other weeds thoroughly over several weeks, if it is applied when they are in active growth. Its action is systemic – that is, it travels through a root system to kill all parts of the plant, but leaves untouched anything else that it has not come into contact with. Systemic weedkillers can be used with great precision among plants that you want to keep, both shrubby and herbaceous.

Tougher weeds, such as ground elder and nettles, need other chemicals. Systemic types are available – ask your garden centre for advice.

Brushwood killers are herbicides that are designed to kill woody plants such as brambles, tree stumps and shrubby species. Needless to say, they should be used with even greater care around shrubs, but they are a very useful tool in the most intractable situations.

Ammonium glyphosate is a very effective herbicide against persistent perennial weeds and woody species; it is systemic and extremely safe, as it breaks down into a completely harmless fertilizer-type chemical after a number of weeks. It is effective but is, unfortunately, expensive.

Whatever chemical you use, make absolutely certain that it is the right one for the job. Follow the instructions on the packet and take all the precautions recommended. Dry sunny days are best for application, which should always be during the growing season, unless instructions are given to the contrary. Windy weather, which will cause spray drift, must be avoided at all costs.

BLACK PLASTIC

Where digging out weeds seems impracticable, because of the scale of the problem, and where you do not wish to use chemicals, the use of a black plastic mulch can work wonders. Heavy-duty black polythene sheeting is spread over the ground, working around any shrubs or plants you wish to keep. It needs to be dug in at the edges and weighted down at intervals. After one summer it can be removed, and the weeds underneath will have been effectively smothered by the lack of light. Any weeds that do come up around wanted plants can be dealt with individually.

If the plastic sheeting cannot be re-used, it should be burned, which it does very cleanly, with no smoke; this is in fact more environmentally responsible than sending it off to a landfill site.

Trees and Shaded Areas

Older borders are often overshadowed by trees, which were all too often planted by previous owners who had no idea that they would get so big. Shade may not necessarily be a problem, given the wide range of interesting and attractive plants that can be chosen, but it may be undesirable, or very deep, or there might be a problem with the tree roots drying out the soil. Now would be a good opportunity to read the chapter on Shade if you have not already done so.

If it seems that the shade is not too hostile an environment and shade-loving plants are an attractive proposition, or perhaps if you want to keep the tree anyway, it should be possible to work around it, perhaps removing the odd branch to let in some more light. Before you start to plan your shaded border, you will need to consider what to do with plants that are currently growing under the tree. Fortunately, most weeds – apart from ground elder – do poorly in shade so they should not be too much of a problem.

Trees in neglected borders often benefit from some tidying up; remove dead or crowded branches or branches that cross over or rub against each other. Fruit trees in particular need careful restorative pruning; you will need to consult an appropriate reference book for advice.

It may seem obvious that a dead tree in a border should be removed, yet this need not necessarily be the case. If there is no evident sign of disease, it may be better to leave it, as it is now recognized that the presence of dead trees can reduce the severity of honey fungus attacks on living trees in the vicinity, by providing a home for other species that compete with the honey fungus. A dead tree also provides a home for a variety of wildlife. Finally, if it is structurally sound – but only if! – it can be a perfect support for climbers. A dead tree may be the only opportunity in many gardens for vigorous climbers, such as rambling roses or the early summer-flowering pink *Clematis montana*, to be allowed to develop their natural size and habit.

Old and misshapen shrubs that have not flowered in ages are a common sight under garden trees. They were planted many years ago, in the fond hope that they would look attractive next to the young tree that had just been planted. There is no point in keeping them if there are no plans to admit more light. If they are retained, they need hard pruning to rejuvenate them (see below).

Dealing with Old Shrubs

The history of the gardening fashions of previous generations can be read by looking at the shrubs left growing in older gardens. Laurels are quintessentially Victorian; evergreen Japanese azaleas date from the 1930s if they are large or from the 1960s onwards if they are smaller; dwarf conifers and heathers date from the 1960s and 1970s. They may be a valuable mature framework for the garden, or a jungle of overgrown monstrosities. Give them time to flower or otherwise prove themselves, then decisions must be made. There are four options: removal, regeneration, hard pruning or leaving them as they are.

Removal

Old shrubs may be cut down and the stumps painted with brushwood killer, which, of course, leaves a huge great stump. The tidy but more labour-intensive alternative is to cut it down and dig out the stump.

Many shrubs have a stump with radiating roots and multiple stems. To prevent regeneration, the entire stump and the larger pieces of root need to be removed. An axe with a long handle is very useful for cutting through the roots, and a crowbar should be used to lever up the stump.

Regeneration

All shrubs can produce new growth from the base – many do so throughout their lives, in fact – while the older stems get woodier and untidier. If the whole thing is cut down to ground level it will regenerate in spring, with healthy vigorous shoots that look a lot more attractive. Old lilacs treated in this way can make more than 2 metres (over 6 feet) of new growth in one year. Good blossom may take a further year.

It is possible to make this an annual operation with a few especially vigorous kinds; elders such as *Sambucus nigra* 'Aurea', for example, are grown for their coloured foliage, which is much better on vigorous young growth.

Borders based on shrubs, like this one, can be very low maintenance, but take a long time to establish and require very careful calculations about the eventual sizes of the plants.

HARD PRUNING

Hard pruning can be undertaken to reshape a shrub, but do not expect much flower until the year after next unless it is carried out right after flowering. This is because most shrubs flower on mature rather than fresh wood.

LEAVING ALONE

The following might be good reasons for keeping a shrub that does not immediately bowl you over:

• the garden would look terribly bare and empty without it;

• it is a good windbreak or screen;

• it is a good barrier in the garden, separating, for example, two parts of the garden from each other;

• it provides a possible nesting site for birds;

• it flowers or looks good at a time when nothing else in the garden does, which allows it at least a temporary reprieve.

Dwarf Shrubs

Small-growing shrubs, such as heathers (*Calluna* and *Erica* spp.) from moorland habitats and many from areas with Mediterranean climates such as lavenders (*Lavandula* spp.), common sage (*Salvia officinalis*) and rock rose (*Cistus* spp.) have a similar habit: low, twiggy and often becoming very woody at the base with age, leading to their losing the attractively hummocky shape they have as younger plants. There are several reasons for this. One is that these plants from harsh environments are kept in better shape in nature because of the effects of the wind, drought or being nibbled by grazing animals. They are

Hardy geraniums, or cranesbills, are very easy plants, and easy to divide too, enabling you to stock other parts of the garden from an initial planting after only a few years.

often burned by seasonal fires, and then regenerate from the base. This is why they need to be clipped regularly in the garden (usually after flowering), the shears taking the place of the grouse or goat.

The distorted specimens of these plants that you see in neglected gardens are often difficult to salvage and some have quite a limited lifespan anyway. Hard cutting back often seems to kill them. Heathers are made of sterner stuff, however, and may be cut back to the base to regenerate them. Replacements should be sought for the others, or cuttings taken, and the old plants pulled out.

Climbers

Elderly climbers are usually large and very tangled. Some, such as Russian vine (*Fallopia baldschuanica*), clematis and honeysuckle (*Lonicera* spp.), may have built up a dense thatch of branches and dead twigs.

Old climbers are often magnificent when in flower, lending a powerful air of romance to the garden. They can, however, be a real nuisance if they are planted in the wrong place or have got so large that they are crushing the arch which was built to support them or the tool shed they were originally planted to hide. Hard cutting back and retraining the main stems to suitably stout supports may be necessary.

Perennials

Herbaceous perennials vary greatly in their longevity and competitiveness, which means that in old borders, especially if they are weed and grass choked, some will have survived, while others will have fallen by the wayside. They present nothing of the problems of removal posed by shrubs, although some seem almost weed-like in their ability to leave behind scraps of regenerating root. Nearly all recover rapidly from replanting, and many also benefit from dividing.

The division of old perennials any time from autumn to early spring is potentially a most valuable source of new plants in a new garden (see the chapter on 'Instant' Gardens, page 124).

The following is a list of the most common survivors in neglected borders. All these plants are long lived, and this list reflects the planting fashions of the previous generation as much as anything.

Anemone × hybrida (syn. *A. japonica*)
Old clumps will flower for many years without particular attention. They are not easy to propagate, though; old growth can be divided in spring but it is slow to re-establish.

Aster
These are very common in older gardens, but many plants may well be seedlings, far inferior to the original varieties. Old clumps are easily divided.

Bergenia (elephant's ear)
A great survivor, but bergenia can suffer from shading from taller vegetation. Clumps are easily divided.

Geranium
Old clumps flower well, but dividing them yields a large number of young plants that are invaluable for rapid filling of newly planted areas. They get woody with age, so division can be hard work.

Hemerocallis (day lily)
Old clumps flower well but are readily divided.

Hypericum calycinum (rose of Sharon)
Common as ground cover and quite voracious of space, if rose of Sharon is thinned out or removed, every last scrap of rhizome must be dug out to prevent regeneration.

Iris
Two kinds are common in older gardens: the broad-leaved, greyish 'bearded' kind, with thick rhizomes at the soil surface, and *I. sibirica*, which forms dense clumps of narrow, fresh green leaves. The former need full sun on the rhizomes to thrive and thus benefit greatly from dividing, and clearing away overshadowing vegetation. *I. sibirica* flowers well as an older plant, but can be divided into a great many smaller ones, although this requires strength.

Leucanthemum × superbum (syn. *Chrysanthemum maximum*; shasta daisy)
This does not survive on all soils, but will benefit from the division of old clumps.

Lysimachia punctata (dotted loosestrife)
Vigorous to the point of being weedy, every scrap of the thicker white roots must be removed if the plant is being taken out. It is good for filling in wild garden areas.

Paeonia (peony)
Peonies are long lived but do not increase well. They take a while to settle down after transplanting – so it is best to leave them alone.

Solidago (golden rod)
Although solidago can be invasive, it is easily reduced in size. The flowers are much appreciated in autumn.

Symphytum (comfrey)
Comfreys are tenacious, with a deep root system that is all but impossible to get rid of without weedkiller or black plastic. Most kinds found in gardens are very dull, but are valued by organic gardeners for liquid manure, because they bring nutrients up from deep in the soil.

Bulbs

Old borders often harbour good numbers of bulbs, such as narcissus, scilla and muscari, which are uncovered during other garden operations. Large clumps may become overcrowded, so thinning them out not only benefits the clumps but provides you with lots more bulbs for free. The best time to dig up most bulbs is soon after they have died down for the summer. Replant in late summer or early autumn; store somewhere cool and dry in the meantime.

The exceptions to the 'move when dormant' rule are cyclamen, snowdrops (*Galanthus* spp.) and winter aconites (*Eranthis hyemalis*), which should be moved 'in the green' – that is, when they are in full growth. With cyclamen this can be done at any time in the winter; with snowdrops and aconites the job should be carried out in late winter, when they are flowering. Dividing the clumps is a finger-numbing job but is rewarded by a greatly increased number of flowers over the next few years.

Left: Established clumps of bulbs are often one of the treasures of older gardens, making it imperative that you 'go carefully' with the spade until you have established where they are.

Replanting Old Borders

Once you have cleared the weeds, removed all the plants you do not want and thinned out others, you will be left with a framework and lots of gaps. How should you go about filling them and what should you choose truly to transform the space, bearing in mind, of course, that you are not starting from scratch but are having to integrate old and new planting so that they complement each other?

The approach taken here is a checklist one, running through all the possible component parts of successful garden borders, briefly noting what they can contribute to one undergoing restoration. More detail on the planting ideas can be found elsewhere in the book, and some case studies are followed up in the next section.

Level One – Structure

- a specimen plant: useful if the border lacks any kind of 'centre of gravity';
- architectural interest: a need for strong forms or distinctive foliage to provide a skeleton for the border;
- evergreens: too many are dreary, but some make all the difference in winter as well as providing continuity;
- shrubs: to fill space, these are the 'bricks and mortar' of mixed borders.

Level Two – Themes

- foliage interest: to provide contrast and continuity;
- colour schemes: plantings often benefit from a disciplined approach to colour;
- coloured foliage: contributing to colour schemes over a longer period than flowers;
- perennials: these are the source of the majority of seasonal change.

Level Three – Ornament

- scent: can one afford to miss out on a whole extra dimension to the border?
- bulbs and annuals: rapidly developing seasonal fillers.

Action plan for revamping an old border

A notebook, drawing and memo approach for an action plan is a good way to tackle an elderly border. The colour scheme for summer to early autumn is mostly pinks, blues and violets, with a limited amount of yellow foliage. All bulbs should be dug out and thinned.

A Cut back to base to regenerate and then keep regularly pruned. There is space in front for perennials (early: *Pulmonaria* spp.; mid-season: blue *Geranium* and *Salvia nemorosa* varieties; late: blue, violet and pink asters). Fill first-season summer gap with annual *Nigella*.

B Remove hydrangea (well past it) and thin out half of kerria, leaving space for new bulbs and small compact shrubs: pink and white rock rose (*Cistus* spp.). Plant five to six rusty foxgloves (*Digitalis ferruginea*) behind for vertical interest. Fill first-season summer gap at front with annual *Nigella*.

C Remove half, divide and use elsewhere, replace with dwarf lavender varieties.

D Cut *Chaenomeles japonica* hard back.

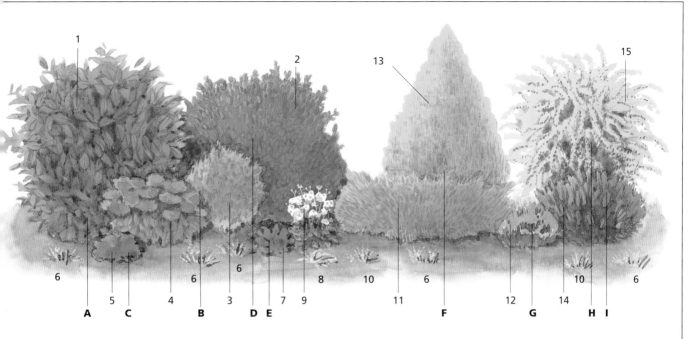

1
2
13
15

6
5
4
3
7 9
8
10
6
11
12
14
6

A
C
B
D E
F
G
H I

E Remove all, thin out drastically and replant. Mix in new bulbs and some ornamental grasses – *Hakonechloa* or *Deschampsia* spp. – for long-season texture.

1. *Prunus laurocerasus*
2. *Chaenomeles japonica*
3. *Kerria japonica*
4. *Hydrangea* variety
5. *Geranium endressii*
6. Bulbs (*Hyacinthoides hispanica*)
7. *Geum* variety
8. Bulbs (*Narcissus* variety)
9. *Anemone* x *hybrida* variety
10. Bulbs (*Crocus* variety)

11. *Juniperus* x *pfitzeriana* 'Pfitzeriana'
12. *Calluna* variety
13. *Thuja occidentalis* 'Rheingold'
14. *Lavandula angustifolia*
15. *Berberis* x *stenophylla*

F Remove misshapen and overgrown conifers and replace with small, rounded specimen tree (*Acer palmatum* variety), planted right at back. Get new bulbs for front. Fill temporary gaps with annual *Cosmos*. Perhaps plant rusty foxglove (*Digitalis ferruginea*) on both sides.

G Remove misshapen heather. Replace with divisions of old *Geranium endressii* and blue-violet asters for later interest. Fill first-season summer gap at front with annual *Nigella*.

H Cut back, remove half and plant herbaceous climber golden hop (*Humulus lupulus* 'Aureus') to scramble over it for summer yellow foliage interest.

I Remove old lavender and replace with small *Miscanthus* grass for winter interest and blue-violet asters for late summer to autumn and as contrast with yellow hop. Add three rusty foxgloves (*Digitalis ferruginea*) to link in with the other group.

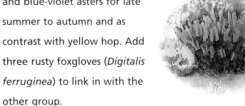

Transforming projects

Having looked at the principles of choosing plants for a variety of different effects, purposes and situations, it is useful to consider some specific projects. All these are based not on the assumption that your garden is a blank slate, but on more realistic garden situations, where there are already trees and shrubs you have not planted yourself or, perhaps, planted long ago and where there are features that you have not planned or built yourself – in other words, where there are things to work around. Seeing for yourself whether these are worth keeping, whether they have potential or not and incorporating them into your plans is all an important part of developing your garden and your garden style.

SMALL FRONT GARDEN IN FULL SUN

This south-facing, hot and dry garden is made worse by the fact that the ground seems more rubble than soil. In addition, it is impossible to water regularly because of the frequency of hosepipe bans, and, because it is the front garden, everyone will see you if you do use a hosepipe!

What is needed

You do want to show off to the rest of the street with something spectacular, but you need a planting that likes sun and does not mind what feels like desert conditions.

SOLUTIONS

Getting rid of the (usually brown) lawn is the first step, so the ground needs to be covered with something, either plants or gravel.

One option is to clothe the ground with low-growing, sun-loving, drought-tolerant Mediterranean plants, which will look very good. You could include, for example, lavender (*Lavandula* spp.), cotton lavender (*Santolina chamaecyparissus*; syn. *S. incana*), rock rose (*Cistus*, *Helianthemum* spp.), broom (*Cytisus* spp.), sage (*Salvia officinalis*), rosemary (*Rosmarinus* spp.) and rue (*Ruta* spp.). They are all evergreen and will mesh together to cover the

A small front garden in full sun

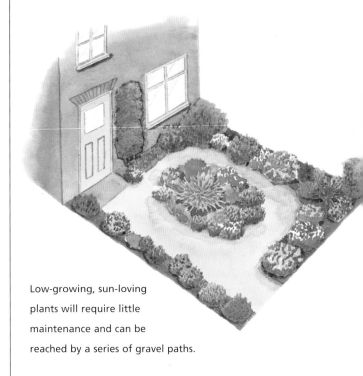

Low-growing, sun-loving plants will require little maintenance and can be reached by a series of gravel paths.

ground and thus need very little care. A small series of stone or gravel paths will allow access for maintenance, which will primarily be clipping. A ceanothus on the rear wall will look truly spectacular in early summer. A specimen yucca provides some 'architecture'. There is no need to 'improve' the soil – doing so would only induce leggy growth (and therefore more clipping) with this kind of plant.

If this solution looks too much like the maquis, then consider a gravel garden. The ground can be covered with gravel and a more limited selection of drought-resistant plants of the kind mentioned above planted through it, so that the gravel comes up to their stems. The more colourful of the above species are chosen.

A gravel garden
can be created by using
some of the more colourful
sun-loving plants and covering
a larger area of the garden with gravel.

SMALL FRONT GARDEN IN SHADE

This garden, which is on the opposite side of the street to the garden on page 144, has the opposite problem – it gets no sun at all. Grass does not flourish, but there is no overhead shade.

What is needed

This garden needs something that not only will look attractive but that will tolerate poor soil and little sunlight.

SOLUTIONS

This is the front garden, so you cannot hide it away as you could if it were round the back. It's there for everyone to see. First, you need to find out where there is most light – this is often at the edge of the shadow of the house – and this is where you can take the opportunity to grow some flowering plants. In the remainder of the garden you may have to use more shade-tolerant but less attractive species. Second, you are going to have to do something to improve the soil if a good variety of plants is to flourish. Compost or well-rotted manure will be needed to get them off to a really good start.

Because the area in light shade is next to the garden wall, some plants will have to be chosen that will reach above it, at least if they are to have any chance of being seen by passers-by. Consider shrubs that are tolerant of light shade, such as the ornamental currant (*Ribes* spp.), *Rubus* 'Benenden' (syn. *R*. Tridel 'Benenden'), aucuba or a common laurel (*Prunus laurocerasus* 'Otto Luyken', for instance), or some of the taller perennials – geraniums, *Campanula persicifolia*, foxgloves (*Digitalis* spp.), aquilegia, hostas, ferns and bergenia, for example.

The darker rear area can be planted with evergreen shade-tolerant foliage plants. A block planting approach, as outlined in the solution to the shady area (see pages 153–4), could be tried, with blocks of the less expensive, easy-to-propagate plants that are tolerant of dry shade, such as periwinkles (*Vinca* spp.), with a few taller, more expensive plants – butcher's broom (*Ruscus aculeata*) or Alexandrian laurel (*Danae racemosa*; syn. *Ruscus racemosus*), for instance – or perhaps the tougher ferns, such as male fern (*Dryopteris filix-mas*), soft shield fern (*Polystichum setiferum*) or hart's tongue fern (*Asplenium scolopendrium*; syn. *Phyllitis scolopendrium*). Perennials for this type of situation include fringecups (*Tellima grandiflora*), pendulous sedge (*Carex pendula*) and woodrush (*Luzula* spp.). Another possibility is a large-growing specimen *Hosta sieboldiana* planted in a container, although you must remember to water it.

If you feel that this approach is too informal for surroundings that are very dominated by bricks and mortar, you could try similar plants in geometric blocks, perhaps contained by low hedges of box (*Buxus* spp.), and possibly with a clipped box specimen in the central area, which might be surrounded by a gravel path. The box centrepiece could be surrounded with a plant such as periwinkle (*Vinca* spp.) or woodrush (*Luzula* spp.), while the smaller area in front, which is also edged with a low box hedge, might contain bergenias, foxgloves (*Digitalis* spp.) and geraniums.

SURROUND TO A TERRACE

For many, the non-gardeners in the family in particular, the terrace is perhaps the most important part of the garden, a place to sit, eat, drink, talk and laze about. The area immediately around it is the backdrop, so it must look good for the whole summer at least, and should smell good, too.

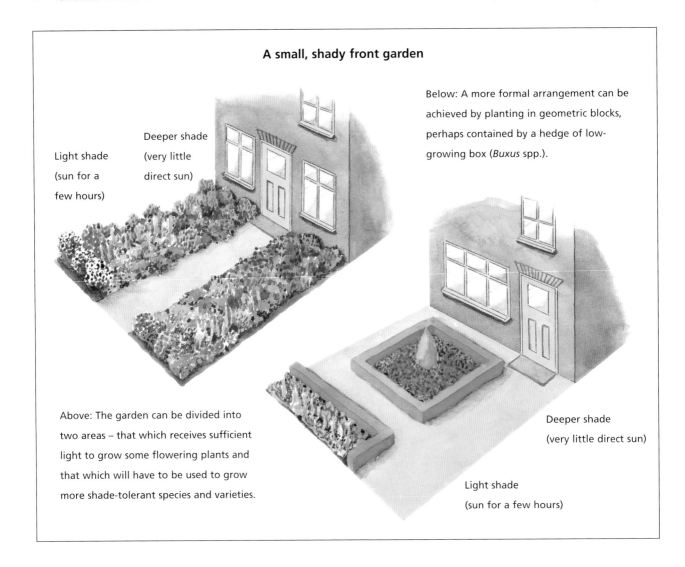

A small, shady front garden

Deeper shade (very little direct sun)

Light shade (sun for a few hours)

Below: A more formal arrangement can be achieved by planting in geometric blocks, perhaps contained by a hedge of low-growing box (*Buxus* spp.).

Above: The garden can be divided into two areas – that which receives sufficient light to grow some flowering plants and that which will have to be used to grow more shade-tolerant species and varieties.

Deeper shade (very little direct sun)

Light shade (sun for a few hours)

In this example, an attractive, sunny terrace has become shaded out by a legacy of inappropriate planting. A number of spring-flowering shrubs have become so large that they are beginning to block the light, quite apart from looking rather dull through the warmer months when the area will be most frequently used. The terrace, which has a balustrade, is raised above the surrounding ground level by about 40cm (16in), so making the use of lower growing plants as part of the terrace surround difficult. There are some steps down to the rest of the garden.

What is needed

Flowers are needed from late spring to autumn, with plenty of scent. Species to attract butterflies are a special request from one family member.

SOLUTIONS

The first step has to be the removal of the larger shrubs to make way for later flowering plants. It may be necessary to replace some of the soil and to improve that in which the shrubs were growing. These are to be replaced by a mixture

The replanted terrace, shown in late summer

Tubs with half-hardy perennials and annuals

1. *Cosmos atrosanguineus*
2. *Lobelia erinus* (white)
3. *Salvia splendens* (maroon-violet)
4. *Osteospermum* 'Buttermilk'
5. *Lobelia erinus* (dark blue)
6. *Verbena* x *hybrida* 'Defiance'
7. *Atriplex hortensis* var. *rubra*
8. *Felicia bergeriana*

9. *Senecio cineraria* (syn. *S. maritimus*)

Climbers

10. *Lonicera periclymenum* 'Belgica'
11. *Lathyrus odoratus*

Perennials flowering from midsummer on

12. *Filipendula rubra*
13. *Macleaya cordata*
14. *Lavatera cachemiriana*

15. *Artemisia lactiflora*
16. *Verbena bonariensis* (syn. *V. patagonica*)

Aromatic plants around steps leading from terrace

17. *Lavandula angustifolia* 'Munstead'
18. *Teucrium chamaedrys*
19. *Ruta graveolens*
20. *Myrtus communis*

of summer-flowering scented shrubs, including some roses. Scented climbers will be planted at the base of the terrace to climb along the top of and through the balustrade.

Further back from the balustrade, late summer- and autumn-flowering perennials will be planted, and these will double up as a border for the neighbouring lawn. They are not especially fragrant, so closeness to the terrace is not important, but all are good for attracting butterflies. Tubs are used for a variety of summer annuals and half-hardy perennials, bringing colour and scent directly into the seating area.

Finally, the steps down to the lawn are surrounded by a variety of lower growing, aromatic plants, which can be touched and smelled by those walking down into the rest of the garden.

NARROW BORDER NEXT TO THE HOUSE

Narrow borders severely limit the creativity of gardeners, often allowing them space to grow what amounts to little more than a row of plants. Where it is impossible to widen the border – perhaps because it is sandwiched between a building and a concrete path – a little imagination is needed to make the most of the available space.

In this garden, a border 40–50cm (16–20in) wide runs along the wall of the house next to a concrete path. The soil is reasonably good.

What is needed

Planting that will bring some sense of life and greenery to a rather bricks-and-mortar environment is required.

A narrow border next to the house

A hot, sun-baked strip along the base of a wall has been planted with *Rosa banksiae* and a honeysuckle (*Lonicera* x *purpusii*) on trellises. The honeysuckle is planted next to the door so that its winter scent may be appreciated. Rue (*Ruta graveolens*), a rock rose (*Cistus* x *purpureus*) and French lavender (*Lavandula stoechas*) fill the border. Gaps can be used for heat-loving dwarf bulbs, such as species tulips and muscari.

A shaded strip border provides rooting for a variegated ivy and the self-clinging, climbing hydrangea (*Hydrangea anomala* subsp. *petiolaris*). At the base are tough shade-lovers, such as bergenia, wood spurge (*Euphorbia amygdaloides* var. *robbiae*; syn. *E. robbiae*), soft shield fern (*Polystichum setiferum*) and hart's tongue fern (*Asplenium scolopendrium*, syn. *Phyllitis scolopendrium*).

The presence of a wall makes the use of climbers as the basis of a planting an obvious solution. Most will need support in the form of trellis or wires against the wall, although some are self-clinging. Choosing suitable climbers should be carried out with care, and two major factors must be considered: size and aspect.

The ultimate size of any climber should be known: triffid-like stems smothering the bathroom window at regular intervals will require all-too-frequent climbing up ladders and pruning. Conversely, a dainty little thing at the foot of a 10m (33ft) wall is plainly inadequate. In addition to the height reached, it is useful to know how far out from the wall the plant will project. Where space is limited, one does not want to be strangled by honeysuckle or impaled on roses.

Aspect is a crucial element in the choice of climbers. Walls facing the sun get very hot, and with a narrow border at the base, the roots will get hot too. Shaded walls offer limited opportunity for flowering climbers, and in these circumstances ivy (*Hedera* spp.) will often be the best choice. 'Foundation planting' at the base of a wall facing the sun or a shaded one will experience similar environmental constraints. Sunny walls are perfect for the kind of Mediterranean shrubs discussed for the sunny front garden (see pages 144–5), and these may indeed be the only ones that can cope with the combination of poor soil and heat often found at the base of a wall. Robust ferns, such as soft shield fern (*Polystichum setiferum*), and perennials, such as bergenia, are more suitable for shadier walls.

NARROW BORDER NEXT TO A FENCE

In this garden a long, narrow border runs between a low fence and a path.

What is needed

Planting is required that will fill the space and look interesting but that will not look like a 'row of plants'.

A narrow fence border

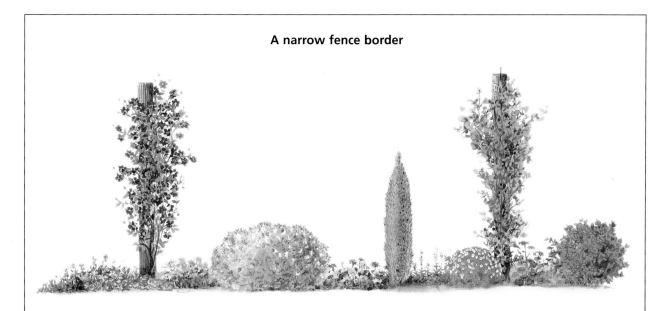

Two climbers, *Clematis* 'Etoile Violette' and the everlasting pea (*Lathyrus grandiflorus*), scramble up two free-standing supports. Irish juniper (*Juniperus communis* 'Hibernica') is another source of vertical interest, while *Hebe rakaiensis* and *Daphne odora* are contrasting clump-forming shapes. Between this framework is a variety of summer half-hardy perennials – varieties of pelargonium, argyranthemum, penstemon and diascia.

SOLUTIONS

The low fence offers little scope for climbers, making this appear to be an even more testing site than the border next to the house wall. However, the soil will probably not be full of foundations and rubble.

The key to making such a border interesting is to provide plenty of variation in form and height, to 'break the line' by adding another, vertical, dimension. The fence is not tall enough to support climbers, so why not erect some fencing posts with wire supports for them (see the chapter on 'Instant' Gardens, page 126). Clump-forming but compact shrubs – shrubby veronicas or *Hebe* spp, for example – will provide a contrast but not occupy too much sideways space. The gaps between these plants can be filled with more insubstantial perennials or annuals.

HOUSE WALL AND ACCOMPANYING BORDER

This garden has a border, some 1.5m (about 5ft) broad, at the foot of a house wall, which experiences sun for half the day. Opportunities for planting would seem limited by the need to keep plants low immediately in front of the windows. This constraint has not, however, deterred the previous resident from planting a buddleia and a large shrub rose, which now threaten to block the windows.

What is needed

Attractive planting is vital so close to the house, and it must have year-round interest but be manageable and predictable.

A border in front of a house wall

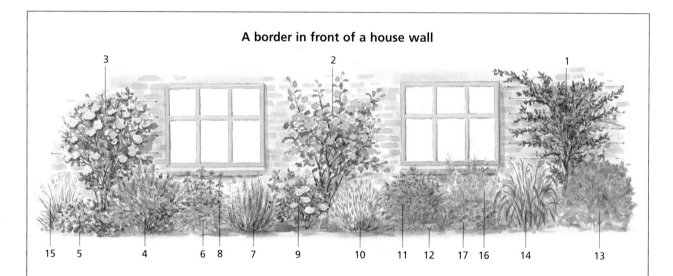

Wall shrubs

1. *Pyracantha* spp., trained to the wall by means of wires
2. *Fremontodendron* spp., not trained to the wall but planted right close up to it
3. *Rosa* 'Constance Spry', supported against the wall by a few wires to strategic stems

Low and compact shrubs

4. *Hebe* 'Midsummer Beauty'
5. *Potentilla fruticosa* 'Abbotswood'
6. *Salvia officinalis* (culinary sage)
7. *Rosmarinus officinalis* (culinary rosemary)
8. *Phlomis italica*
9. *Rosa* 'Louise Odier'
10. *Lavandula angustifolia*
11. *Spiraea japonica* 'Anthony Waterer'
12. *Thymus vulgaris* (culinary thyme)
13. *Ceanothus* x *delileanus* 'Gloire de Versailles'

Grasses

14. *Miscanthus sinensis* 'Graziella'
15. *Molinia caerulea* subsp. *caerulea* 'Heidebraut'

Perennial

16. *Perovskia atriplicifolia*

Annual flowers for cutting

17. *Nigella* spp. and *Consolida* spp.

The buddleia is an example of a plant that is completely unsuitable for such a situation: it is incredibly vigorous, making up to 2m (over 6ft) of growth in a year. It must be removed. The rose is probably worth keeping, because it could be hard pruned every winter to restrict its growth.

What has been said about climbers against a wall (see page 148) is valid here, although there is plenty of scope for varieties that project further out from the wall. Large shrubs are definitely out, although some could be trained as wall shrubs (see the chapter on Assessing Your Garden, page 25). The example here uses medium sized, neatly growing shrubs and perennials, and, where windows reach down low, only predictably compact or prostrate varieties are used.

Because it is close to the house, this might be a good place for 'useful' plants – herbs, cut flowers or even salad vegetables, for example – and some of these are included here as well.

OVERGROWN ISLAND BED

Island beds come in many shapes and sizes and occur in many different types of location. Here we look at two commonly occurring situations where bad planting has created several problems.

In the first example, an island bed has been planted with a mixture of shrubs that are too close together. This has created a formless thicket in the midst of which several smaller varieties are more or less crushed by the other larger specimens. The existing shrubs have all finished

---

A replanted island bed shown in late summer

Areas outlined in red are newly planted

Existing shrubs

1. *Choisya ternata*
2. *Mahonia* x *media* 'Buckland'
3. *Cotinus coggygria* 'Royal Purple'
4. *Chaenomeles speciosa*
5. *Berberis* x *stenophylla*
6. *Hydrangea macrophylla* 'Blue Wave'

New planting

7. *Malus tschonoskii*
8. *Aster lateriflorus* 'Horizontalis'

9. *Geranium* 'Spinners'
10. *Hakonechloa macra*
11. *Eupatorium purpureum* 'Purple Bush'
12. *Achillea* 'Lachsschönheit'
13. *Geranium clarkei* 'Kashmir White'
14. *Thalictrum aquilegiifolium*

15. *Carex muskingumensis*
16. *Bergenia* 'Sunningdale'
17. *Bergenia* 'Silberlicht'
18. *Geranium endressii*
19. *Aster cordifolius*
20. *Anemone* x *hybrida* 'Honorine Jobert'

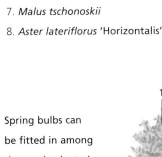

Spring bulbs can be fitted in among the newly planted perennials, with some additional sites in gaps around the edges.

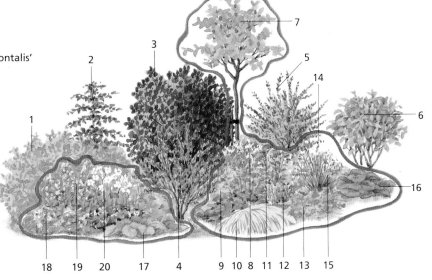

flowering by early summer. The bed is in a key position, so it is important that it looks good for most of the year at the very least.

What is needed

A longer season of interest is required, but with something that will give a sense of structure during the winter months.

SOLUTIONS

The existing shrubs need to be thinned ruthlessly, removing about half of them to provide more space for the survivors and for some additional, later season planting. The least worthy should be taken out, while the larger remaining ones should be cut hard back. A couple of smaller shrubs, which are badly misshapen as a result of being crushed by the larger ones, now have enough space to develop fully; they are cut down to ground level to allow them to regenerate and develop a healthy shape. Several gaps are created to allow for additional planting.

Space for a small specimen tree on the main axis of the bed, but off-centre, is created. This will create a good all-year centre of gravity for the bed.

Three bays are created for the planting of medium to tall, mid- to late summer-flowering perennials. Compost and fertilizer are used to improve the soil.

Additional areas at the edge of the bed are created for early- to midsummer low-growing perennials and autumn- to spring-flowering bulbs. These will provide an edging for the bed. Where there is no space, or not likely to be space in the next few years because of expected shrub growth, the bed is extended slightly outwards to accommodate the perennials and bulbs.

CONIFER-FILLED ISLAND BED

The second problem that is often found with island beds is a humpbacked bed on an exposed site in an area of infertile acid soils, that was planted around 20 years ago by someone with a mania for dwarf conifers. Many are now no longer dwarf, and if there ever was anything else in the bed, it has vanished without trace.

What is needed

(Apart from a chainsaw and a bonfire site, that is.) Mature dwarf and low-growing conifers can make fine plants – if they have space. Thinning is needed to create this space and to make some space for other plants that will provide flowers and appear less rigid than the conifers.

SOLUTIONS

The most out-of-proportion conifers are taken out, together with any prostrate varieties that have covered too large an area of ground. It is important that the shapes of those remaining seem to be in proportion and to have harmony, and it may be necessary to remove more in order to achieve this. The stumps and major roots of the removed plants should be dug out, and some additional local topsoil brought in to make up the soil levels.

Substantial gaps are now left, and these can be filled in three stages. First, a variety of heathers, which will provide flower and foliage colour throughout the year, is used as the basis for the new planting. Dwarf and compact rhododendrons are also added.

Next, some ornamental grasses are added to create a sense of movement and for winter interest. Finally, spring bulbs can be added if space is left for them to develop without being covered by the heathers. There will be some space around the grasses in spring. Additional small gaps for them can be made, but these will benefit from covering with wood mulch to help prevent weed incursion when the bulbs have finished.

A replanted island bed on acid soil shown in late winter

Existing plants

1. *Juniperus chinensis* 'Stricta'
2. *Picea abies* 'Ohlendorffii'
3. *Chamaecyparis lawsoniana* 'Gnome'
4. *Thuja orientalis* 'Aurea Nana'

New planting

5. *Deschampsia cespitosa* 'Bronzeschleier'
6. *Calluna vulgaris* 'Gold Haze'
7. *Calluna vulgaris* 'Multicolor'
8. *Molinia caerulea* 'Dauerstrahl'
9. *Erica carnea* 'Vivellii'
10. *Erica cinerea* 'Eden Valley'
11. *Rhododendron* 'Elizabeth'
12. *Rhododendron yakushimanum*
13. *Molinia caerulea* subsp. *caerulea* 'Moorhexe'

SHADY AREA

A large sycamore (*Acer pseudoplatanus*) overshadows what was once a shrub border and part of a lawn, while a birch (*Betula* spp.) stands almost adjacent to it. The lawn is practically dead under the sycamore and is thin under the birch. Frequent walking between the two is rapidly reducing the 'grass' to a mud-bath. The shrubs have been distorted in their attempt to reach light and have, in any case, become shapeless and unattractive.

What is needed

The first requirement is a replacement for the grass – something that can be walked on and is shade tolerant. Next, ground cover is needed to replace other areas of grass. This should look more attractive and tolerate both light and deep shade. Something shrub-like in scale should be included to provide some screening; it will have to tolerate shade and the drying of the soil caused by the sycamore roots. Finally, plants that will grow better in shade are needed to take the place of some of the shrubs in the border.

SOLUTIONS

Stepping-stones can be walked on and are remarkably shade tolerant. No plant exists that withstands both foot traffic and deep shade.

The range in light levels, from quite bright to deep shade, can be treated together if a low-maintenance, very tidy effect is wanted. Blocks of planting can be woven around among the stepping-stones: swirls of dark green, evergreen sedge (*Carex* spp.) and woodrush (*Luzula* spp.) look like 30–40cm (12–16in) high coarse grass (but never need

A shady area

The green line indicates the outer edges of the tree canopies and, hence, the outer limit of the darkest shade.

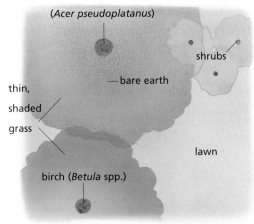

sycamore
(*Acer pseudoplatanus*)

shrubs

— bare earth

thin, shaded grass

lawn

birch (*Betula* spp.)

Stepping-stones and more a thoughtful selection of ground-cover plants transform what was a rather unattractive area.

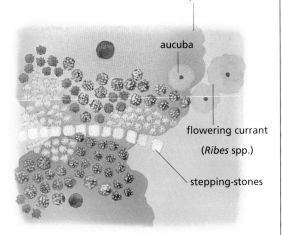

former shrubs, now replaced by taller, shade-tolerant perennials

aucuba

flowering currant (*Ribes* spp.)

stepping-stones

 = *Carex pendula*

= *Luzula* spp.

= *Vinca* spp.

= *Geranium* 'Claridge Druce'

cutting). Other evergreen ground-cover plants, such as periwinkles (*Vinca* spp.) produce some flower, while the semi-evergreen geranium produces attractive flowers.

Alternatively, the dark foliage ground cover can be restricted to the deepest shade and the lighter shade of the geranium planted in a more fluid and naturalistic style, mixed with a selection of other shade-tolerant plants, which will flower on and off throughout the summer.

Buying in ground cover on this scale is obviously formidably expensive, but all these plants are easily propagated by division from stock plants more than two years old. All, except for the periwinkle, can be produced in even larger numbers from self-saved seed, and the plant will be large enough for planting out after a year.

The existing shrubs look in too bad a state to be saved. An exception is an aucuba, which is shade tolerant, but it was planted too close to other more vigorous species. Cut it back and feed it and, with luck, it will regenerate itself and be able to make the most of having more space around it. Plant a flowering currant (*Ribes sanguineum*) on the lighter side, to provide some additional screening.

In the site vacated by the old shrubs there is possibly enough light for a variety of plants that will tolerate light shade. The soil will be impoverished by the shrubs, so compost and some fertilizer should be dug in before replanting. Some true shade-lovers are selected and mixed with a couple – aquilegia and foxgloves (*Digitalis* spp.) – that need more light but that have the ability to self-seed, allowing them to spread to where they feel happiest.

SMALL POND

Small ponds are immensely popular in gardens, but they can create a legacy of unwanted concrete and plastic for the new owners. The sheer difficulty of removing them often means that they are retained. Rather than this being a negative decision, it is important that if the pond is kept then every effort is made to incorporate it attractively into the rest of the garden. 'Incorporate' is the operative word here; too often garden ponds bear absolutely no relation to their surroundings. What informally shaped ponds need more than anything else is context – that is, accompanying wetland plants.

In this garden, a leaking concrete pond, 3 × 1 × 2m (10 × 3 × 6ft), is choked with overgrown water plants. The accompanying 'rockery' – that is, a pile of stones – stands to one side of the garden, isolated from the rest of the garden by lawn.

What is needed

A naturalistic water feature should be surrounded by attractive vegetation that blends into the rest of the garden.

SOLUTIONS

The first problems are practical: to drain the pond and remove all vegetation and then to clean it out and mend the leaks. The rockery is removed.

It is decided to start again with new pond plants, carefully choosing varieties that are small growing and will not, therefore, abuse your hospitality. To develop a context for the pond, it should to be surrounded by plants to create a sense of there being waterside vegetation. Taller, shrubby

plants are to be used to the rear of the pond, to provide a backdrop and further context.

Pond plants need to be carefully researched in order to find varieties that will not get too big, and it is well worth going to specialist water plant nurseries rather than to garden centres.

Waterside plants need water, but because this is a concrete pond, the soil outside the pond will be no moister than the rest of the garden. As long as it is not too dry, however, species can be chosen that look as if they are natural waterside ones, and a good many marsh plants are happy in normal garden conditions anyway, and do not require specifically damp conditions.

At the rear of the pond some larger ornamental grasses, such as the versatile *Miscanthus sinensis*, are planted to look like reeds, together with some willows (*Salix* spp.) to create the illusion of marshland. The willows have attractively coloured stems in the winter, but they must be pruned to the base every other year (otherwise they will get rather too big for many gardens).

A replanted pond and surrounding area shown in midsummer

Small-growing aquatic and marginal plants
1. *Menyanthes trifoliata*
2. *Nymphaea odorata*
3. *Nymphaea* 'Pygmaea'
4. *Typha minima*
5. *Acorus calamus* 'Variegatus'
6. *Caltha palustris*

Plants for accompanying 'wetland' area
7. *Iris pseudacorus*
8. *Iris sibirica*
9. *Rodgersia pinnata* 'Superba'
10. *Hosta* 'Blue Angel'
11. *Eupatorium purpureum*
12. *Miscanthus sinensis* 'Silberfeder'
13. *Salix alba* subsp. *vitellina* 'Britzensis' ('stooled' or cut back to ground level every year)
14. *Filipendula rubra*

INDEX

Page numbers in italic refer to the illustrations

Abutilon 123
Acer palmatum 84
acid soils 110–12
Actinidia kolomikta 24
Aegopodium podagraria 135
Agave 67
Ajuga reptans 120
Akebia quinata 132
alkaline soils 112–13
Allium giganteum 109
Aloysia triphylla 93
Amelanchier canadensis 65, *65*
ammonium glyphosate 136
Anemone
  A. blanda 23, 101, *101*
  A. hybrida 102, 139
Angelica archangelica 66
annuals
  colour 127, 133
  containers 118
  cottage-garden 76
  flower cycles 71
  half-hardy 127, *128*
  hardy 76
Antirrhinum 120
aquatic plants 155, *155*
Araucaria araucana 64
Arbutus 64
architectural plants 46–59,
  46–56, 58, 115
  see also specimen plants
Argyranthemum
  foeniculaceum 121
Arundo donax 59
Asplenium scolopendrium 101
assessment, gardens 14–27
Aster 84, 139
  A. divaricatus 102
  A. 'Little Carlow' *16*, 84
  A. macrophyllus 102
  x *frikartii* 'Mönch' *84*
Astilbe 99
autumn
  bulbs 77
  coastal gardens *110*

colour 33–4, *39*, 68, *69*, 73, 84–5
exposure *108*
soils 106, *106*, 112, *112*, 113, *113*
waterlogging 104, *105*

bamboo 97
bare patches 23–5, *23*
bedding plants 127, *128*
Bergenia 54, 57, 139
berries 72, 78–9
Betula 65
black plastic 136
block planting 97
blues 28, *29*, 31, *35*, 38–9, 42
borders
  architectural plants 46–54
  assessing 14–17, *15, 16*
  colour 6, 14–16, *16,*
   28–39, *28–40*
  house walls 150–1, *150*
  narrow 148–50, *148–50*
  old 26, 134–43, *134,*
   137–8, 140–3
  specimen plants 61–3
Brachyscome iberidifolia 121
brambles 135
bronze foliage 37
Brugmansia arborea 123, *123*
Brunnera macrophylla 29
Buddleja 129
bulbs
  borders 140–1, 141
  colour 125, *125*
  containers 118, *119*
  continuity 74, *75*, 77, *80–1*
  dry soils 106
  exposure 109
  fragrance 89
  waterlogging 105
Buxus spp. 46–7, *47, 48*, 58
buying plants 11–13

calendars (gardens) *80–1*
Calendula officinalis 83
Calomeria amaranthoides 93

Caltha palustris 82, *82*
Canna 67
Carex 45, 122
Ceanothus 127, *127*, 129, *129*
Centaurea cyanus 133
choosing plants 8, 11–13, 33–4,
  63, 115–18, *117–19*
Chusquea culeou 64
Cimicifuga 102–3, *103*
Clarkia amoena 133
Clematis
  C. armandii 59
  C. cirrhosa 85
  C. montana 117, *126,*
   132, *132*
  C. orientalis 132
  C. tangutica 132
climate 13
climbers
  containers 116, *118*
  continuity 75–6
  fast-growing 125–6, *126, 128,*
   132–3, *132*
  fragrance 90
  hiding areas 26
  old 139
  shrubs 20
  walls 25, *148–9*, 149–50
clipped trees 46–8, 58–9
coastal gardens 109–10
cold 13, 108–9, 116
colour 28–45, *28–41, 43–4*
  annuals 127, 133
  autumn 33–4, *39*, 68, *69,*
   73, 84–5
  borders 6, 14–16, *16,*
   28–39, *28–40*
  containers *24*
  cool 30, 38
  foliage *8–9, 16*, 28, 32, *32,*
   34–8, *34–7, 39*, 44–5
  hot 30, 31–2, *32, 39*
  instant 125, *125*, 127
  ornamental grasses 74
  pastel 30–1, *30–1, 38*, 42

PHOTOGRAPH ACKNOWLEDGEMENTS

Jonathan Buckley 1 (Dolwen, Llanrhaeadr, Nr. Oswestry), 2 (Great Dixter, East Sussex), 6 (Helen Yemm's Garden, London, SW17), 16 (Great Dixter, East Sussex), 35 (The Dingle, Welshpool, Powis), 41 (17 Morden Rd Mews, London, SE3), 47 (Green Farm Plants, Hampshire), 50 (Green Farm Plants, Hampshire), 61 (The Dingle, Welshpool, Powis), 63 (White Windows, Hampshire), 65 (The Dingle, Welshpool, Powis), 66 (Beth Chatto Gardens, Essex), 72 (East Ruston Old Vicarage, Norfolk), 78–79 (Great Dixter, East Sussex), 84 (The Hiller Garden), 87 (5 Burbage Rd, London, SE24), 92 (Janey Lloyd Owen's Garden, Wandsworth), 93 (Wisley), 95 (Abbey Dore, Herefordshire), 115 (Mrs Hatchard's Garden, Nr Welshpool), 126 (Crystal Palace Rd, London), 127 (Helen Yemm's Garden, London, SW17), 130 (The Hiller Garden); **Jerry Harpur** 30 (Sun House, Suffolk), 62 (Sun House, Suffolk), 95 (Inverewe, Scotland), 96 (Inverewe, Scotland), 97 (Beth Chatto Gardens, Essex), 105 (Design: Oehme & van Sweden, Washington DC), 109 (Design: Oehme & van Sweden, Washington DC), 114 (Beth Chatto Gardens, Essex), 123 (Peter Wooster, Conn, USA); **Marcus Harpur** 29 (Chenies Manor, Bucks), 125 (Chenies Manor, Bucks), 135 (Chiffchaffs, Dorset), 140 (Chiffchaffs, Dorset); **Anne Hyde** 8–9 (Brian Cross, 'Lakemount', Co. Cork, Ireland), 10 (Chris Hubbard, St Johns Rd, Hitchin, Herts), 11 (Mr & Mrs Metson, Coverwood Lakes, Surrey), 12–13 (Mr & Mrs Metson, Coverwood Lakes, Surrey), 14 (Forde Abbey, Somerset), 15 (Forde Abbey, Somerset), 19 (Forde Abbey, Somerset), 22 (Ruth Thornton, Balfour Rd, Northampton), 23 (Mrs Willis, Ivy Lodge, Radway, Warks), 24 (Spindrift, Jordans, Bucks), 28 (Dr Ruth Chippindale, High Street, Harlton, Cambs), 36 (Dr Ruth Chippindale, High Street, Harlton, Cambs), 46 (Cecilia Gonzalez, Ellesmere Gardens, Essex), 47 (Mr J. Drake, Hardwicke House, Fen Ditton, Cambs), 49 (Cecilia Gonzalez, Ellesmere Gardens, Essex), 54 (Malley Terry, Hillgrove Crescent, Kidderminster), 55 (Judy Brown, Masham Manor, Surrey), 60 (Geoffrey Verey Esq., 'Little Bowden', Berks), 64 (Jon Tye, Lea Gardens, Derbys), 69 (Mr & Mrs Sadler, Halfpenny Furze, Chalfont-St-Giles, Bucks), 98 (Mr & Mrs Bennett, Lavender Hill, Enfield), 102 (Faith Raven, Docwras Manor, Shepreth, Cambs), 111 (Jon Tye, Lea Gardens, Derbys), 117 (Pascoe, Pinn Way, Ruislip); **Andrew Lawson** 18 (Gothic House, Oxon), 21 (Gothic House, Oxon), 29 (Bosvigo House, Cornwall), 32 (Bosvigo House, Cornwall), 34, 43, 44, 58, 68, 69, 70 (Designer: Wendy Lauderdale), 82, 84, 86 (Chilcombe House, Dorset), 87 (Chilcombe House, Dorset), 88–89 (Alderley Grange, Glos.), 91, 94, 101, 103, 104, 107 (Beth Chatto Gardens, Essex), 115, 119, 121, 122, 124 (Gothic House, Oxon), 125, 129, 131, 134, 137 (Hodges Barn, Glos.), 138 (Owslebury, Hants.), 145 (Owslebury, Hants.); **Tony Lord** 15 (Heslington Manor); **Juliette Wade** 56, 132.